Sifting Artifacts

Endowed by

TOM WATSON BROWN

and

THE WATSON-BROWN FOUNDATION, INC.

Sifting Artifacts

Kathy A. Bradley

MERCER UNIVERSITY PRESS
Macon, Georgia

MUP/ P642

© 2022 by Mercer University Press
Published by Mercer University Press
1501 Mercer University Drive
Macon, Georgia 31207
All rights reserved

25 24 23 22 21   5 4 3 2 1

Books published by Mercer University Press are printed on acid-free paper that meets the requirements of the American National Standard for Information Sciences—Permanence of Paper for Printed Library Materials.

Printed and bound in the United States.

This book is set in Adobe Caslon Pro.

Cover/jacket design by Burt&Burt.

ISBN   978-0-88146-834-2
eBook   978-0-88146-835-9
Cataloging-in-Publication Data is available from the Library of Congress

Also by Kathy Bradley

Breathing and Walking Around

Wondering Toward Center

In Which the Metaphor Makes Itself Known

Echocardiogram.

I am lying on my side. Most of my chest is exposed. It is dotted with white circles. Attached to the white circles are cables trailing away from me—twisting and falling and coiling like the tentacles of an octopus—on their way toward a computer monitor.

The technician is pleasant, if intent. Her hands among the wires remind me of a harpist.

"There we go," she mumbles to herself. "There we are. There it is."

There, there, there, I tell myself in the voice that comforts frightened children. It will be fine, I tell myself in the voice I use to convince judges and juries. There, there, there. No reason to be alarmed. No reason to be concerned. This is all cautionary.

Cautionary. I've spent most of my life exercising caution—slowing for yellow lights, thinking twice, watching my steps. I've never leapt before I looked. I've never put all my eggs in one basket. I've never rocked any boat or upset any apple cart. Surely all that caution will pay off here. Here in this cold room where all my thoughts have turned into simple declarative sentences.

The technician—I notice now how young she is—ignores the nest of wires and cables and concentrates on the monitor. By twisting my neck and looking up and back over my shoulder, I can see blurred images of fluttering movement, like those on our black and white television that always took a few seconds to come into focus.

Her shoulders round and her eyes squint just a bit at the image floating in the center of the screen. The thing is pulsing. The beat is regular—Ta-dump. Ta-dump. The shape, though, is not regular. It is amorphous, the very definition of shapeless. It is a throbbing mass of flesh and blood and electrical impulses. It is my heart.

I start doing math in my head. I am good at that, doing math in my head. I figure that, as of today, my heart has beat almost three billion times. Three *billion* times.

The echocardiogram is only the first of many tests. When they are all over—when all the lying still one moment, walking briskly the next is over, when all the assorted measuring resulting from the half-apologetic mention to my internist of the sudden, unusual, prolonged stabbing pain in the center of my chest is over—I am sitting in a room waiting for the doctor. I am reading *Lincoln in the Bardo*. It does not occur to me at the time that there is something slightly macabre in the coincidence of my reading material.

The doctor comes in, rifling through papers on a clipboard. He smiles, shakes my hand, introduces himself, and sits down. I am prepared. I think.

"Everything looks good," he says.

I am a little startled. I am sure he can see it on my face. I suspect that he has learned how to read faces in his line of work. "All the tests look good. Your blood pressure and heart rate are normal. You did fine on the stress test. The EKG looks good."

I can feel myself beginning to relax. The various mantras I've been reciting to myself are fading into the distance like a marching band that has rounded the corner. Everything looks good. Nothing wrong. Deep breath.

"There is, though, one thing."

And for a moment the room goes quiet. And still. And black. As does the world. My world. The bullet that I thought, for the briefest of moments, I had dodged has defied the laws of physics and, like something shot out of a cartoon gun, has reversed its trajectory and is whizzing its way back toward me. I am the target silhouette at the gun range, immobile and incapable of defense.

Still, the young doctor is smiling. He is not avoiding my gaze. He hasn't asked if I have anyone with me. These, the constant optimist in me thinks, could be good signs.

I will never stop being amazed at the human brain and its ability to construct and tell itself a story—complete with plot, conflict, climax, and resolution—all within the span of five seconds.

"There is, though, one thing. There was a little something that showed up on the nuclear stress test, but it doesn't appear to be affecting the blood flow to your heart." He glances down at his papers. Is he reading something? Or is my unblinking stare making him uncomfortable?

He looks back up. "A number of things can cause something like this to appear, any number of things that can cause an unusual spike or dip in the reading. Maybe you moved just the least little bit and that kept the equipment from getting a perfect image."

I resist the urge to correct him, to assure him that I did not move, not the least little bit, that I in no way failed to follow the instructions given to me in every room, connected to every machine.

"Or," he continues, "it could be a tiny piece of blood vessel that came loose and is floating around. We call it an artifact. And," he pauses in response to my eyes getting wider, "it's not going to kill you."

An artifact.

He keeps talking. And smiling. He tells me to carry baby aspirin with me for the unlikely moment that I experience the pain again. He makes sure I understand that I should get to the hospital immediately if it does. He mentions regular follow-up visits just to check on things. He assures me that, in his opinion, my heart is completely healthy and I have nothing to worry about.

I hear him, but I am hardly listening. My brain, with neural pathways trained to find connection everywhere, taught since sometime around fourth grade to search for symbolism in every word and phrase, schooled by circumstance and experience to believe that randomness does not exist, is stuck on "We call it an artifact."

And, suddenly, in this very stark and clinical setting, this moment heavy with tension, I am trying not to laugh. Trying not to startle this very earnest young man, bringing to bear all his training and expertise to make sure that I understand the serious, but not grave, information he is sharing, by emitting a loud guffaw.

Because, of course, it is called an artifact. This thing, this phantom, this marker on my heart. This leftover from a previous time, long hidden but never gone.

And you are correct, dear doctor. It is not going to kill me. It tried, but it did not succeed.

I remember enough social studies and I've seen enough Indiana Jones movies to know what an artifact is. I know that archaeologists use topographic maps and transits, twine and pegs, trenches and trowels and augers to find them. I know they use a shaker screen to separate what they find from the soil in which it is encased, that they shake it back and forth, freeing the dirt to pass through the mesh and leave behind an artifact, sometimes as small as a quarter of an inch. The use of a shaker screen, I remind myself, is a solitary job.

I have a friend who studied to be an archaeologist. I interviewed him once. He told me about working with a famous treasure hunter in the Florida Keys in the discovery of a Spanish galleon lost at sea. "There is a thrill," he told me, "that comes with uncovering something from the past." But, he explained, the thrill is not the point of the search. And neither are the objects themselves, the items raised from the sea or dug from the ground.

The purpose, he explained, is to listen for and then try to answer the questions that call out from the coins, the bowl, the bones. "Whose hands held this? Made this? Why were they here? What did they think? What became of them?"

It is not simply what you find. It is what you find out.

There is a single characteristic shared by every writer I know. It is the automatic, involuntary, default thought process that turns a new word, either never heard before or heard in a new context, into—at the least bothersome—an object of intense curiosity or—at the most intense—a hounding metaphor.

In the days after my visit to the cardiologist, "artifact" becomes a hounding metaphor.

I am pursued like a gazelle by a cheetah. I close my eyes to sleep and my brain begins digging, shaking. A memory appears: an insignificant event punctuated by innocuous words, now recognized as the source of an expression, a bit of body language, a repetitive response that is part of who I am twenty, forty, sixty years later. Or I hear music I've not heard in years and I am suddenly feeling the emotions, long suppressed, associated with the time and place when I last heard those lyrics, that melody.

I am, without knowing it at first, becoming an archaeologist of my own life. Anything—a phrase in a book, a voice on television, a glimpse in the rear-view mirror as I change lanes—can set me digging. Shoveling with care, shaking the screen gently, and watching the dirt fall away, I am uncovering artifacts.

Humans are natural archaeologists. We search for the shards and bone fragments that remain in the soil where our past lives were lived, employing the same methods and tools as scientists. We map the years with photographs and yearbooks and stories told around dinner tables. We stake the people and places that we claim as our own. We dig into the darkness, below the surface, by remembering, by calling up the moments of celebration and disappointment, of accomplishment and heartbreak, of contentment and chaos.

I have spent much of my life searching, mostly for the right words but also for the right time, the right choice, the right person. It is because I have understood without ever saying, ever articulating, ever *being able to articulate* that nothing just happens. It happens and it leaves something behind, like a trace element. And what is left behind is never gone.

In the aftermath of the stressing and measuring and photographing of my heart, the searching has become more pointed. I now dig a little deeper and stare a little harder in hope of unearthing an artifact, finding something I didn't know was there, something of which I can ask a question, from which I can find an answer.

Pencil and paper are primitive tools, but they are the ones I know. They are the ones that I use to engage in the sifting that will unearth questions worth asking and the answers worth clutching like a life raft. They are my shaker screen, the means by which I take the disturbed earth and remove from it small things of value, quarter-inch truth.

"The only questions that really matter are the ones you ask yourself."
—Ursula K. LeGuin

JANUARY 11, 2015

It may have been the trees, soaring and spreading and stretching up into the sky and down into the earth. It may have been the words, carved into stone in letters thick and straight, their assertion of permanence both ironic and inspiring. It may have been the silence or the stillness or the statuary that captivated me, that made the cemetery at Christ Church on Saint Simons Island one of my favorite places. I don't remember and I can't say that I ever knew for certain, but on that day the thing that grabbed me and held me was the camellias.

On that day, five days after Christmas, with the tree still up and a handful of presents still to be delivered, I had driven the back roads—Sandhill to Claxton to Glennville to Ludowici to Townsend to Darien to Saint Simons—to catch my breath and refocus my gaze. And I'd brought a friend along, someone who'd heard me talk about this spit of land that holds so much of me and my heart and wanted firsthand knowledge. We had gone in search of Tree Spirits. We had breathed in salt air and strolled past sand dunes and tidal pools from the Coast Guard Station to Gould's Inlet and back to Massengale Park. And now we had come to Christ Church.

On a brick path worn smooth by two hundred years of footsteps, we circled the church to enter the cemetery. No gates or fences. No separation of the dead from the living. We wandered slowly among the graves—old, extremely old, and new, elaborate and humble. I pointed out to my friend a broken column, monument to a life cut short, the one piece of funerary art I knew.

I made the comment that wandering through graveyards had been a regular pastime in my childhood, something that the aunts and cousins always did on Thanksgiving afternoon while the men played pitch penny in the backyard or drove out to somebody's pond to throw a line. My friend didn't say anything, but the expression I got in response made me think that people in Ohio didn't do that kind of thing.

At the corner of one plot, there was a large camellia bush. It had grown tall, like a tree, and its branches dangled over the path. The pink flowers and dark green leaves stood out against the gray day, the gray stones. My friend pointed and said, "Rose?"

"Camellia," I corrected, not realizing right away how odd it must be for someone from Ohio to see such a profusion of blooms in the dead of winter, not realizing right away, even, how odd it was for me to respond so quickly. I am not known for my horticultural expertise.

I plucked one blossom from the bush and held it in my upturned palm. Chamois soft and the color of a teenager's first crush blush, petals falling away from the center like the skirt of a ball gown. Both shy and brave, tender and strong. Alive and vibrant and animated in this place that bears witness to death.

The sign at the gate read "Open until sunset," and the sun had already fallen behind the trees that separated the church from the Frederica River and the marsh. It was time to go.

I walked toward the car with my hand up like Mr. Carson in *Downton Abbey*, cradling the camellia and thoughts I had not yet begun to process.

There was just enough light to walk to the Wesley Cross before heading back to the village for dinner before driving home, this time the back roads in reverse—Saint Simons to Darien to Townsend to Ludowici to Glennville to Claxton to Sandhill. The car was dark and the talk serious. The camellia lay in the cupholder between us.

It is cold outside tonight. Jaw-locking, teeth-clinching, head-bowing cold. The forecast is for temperatures as low as 19 degrees. I am worried for the camellias. All over town they have been bursting forth and showing off. Pink and red and coral. Stripes and solids. Ruffles and flounces. In the morning, they will be stiff and brittle and dead. I am imagining the ones at Christ Church Cemetery falling from their stems to the brick paths below.

Everything dies. In winter it is just more difficult to deny. This winter I am thinking that before my turn comes I want to be like the camellias, blooming with a flagrancy that would embarrass my younger self, blooming in places flush with darkness and death, blooming to bear witness to all I have been, all I have known, all I have loved.

JANUARY 25, 2015

From inside the house I can hear both sets of wind chimes clanging, harmonizing from opposite eaves, dancing madly like Russian Cossacks. The sun is high and the light is white. There is no good reason to stay inside.

The ruts in the road have dried into peaks, crunchy beneath the footfalls that I am trying unsuccessfully to slow to a stroll. I am wondering: Is this sky really the bluest sky I've ever seen? Or am I just so glad, so astonished, so grateful that the clouds have been driven away and the gray swept aside that anything close to blue would seem bluest?

To the crossroads and back is 1.8 miles. To the highway and back is 3.9. There is easily enough daylight left for the longer trek. My legs need stretching. My mind needs clearing. I will take the long way.

And then, just as I get to the grain bins, just as the road begins to fall down the hill toward the red clay alley of pine trees, I change my mind. I leave the road and step over the shallow ditch into the field, littered with cotton stalks matted by days of rain.

The fencerow that marks its boundary is not even a fencerow anymore, the wire and posts long gone, but it is along the fencerow that I walk, on a bed of autumn's pine needles, that my feet finally lose their rush.

I didn't bring a clip for my hair, and the wind that is whipping across the field, that has gained speed and force over the flatness of nearly a hundred acres, has me tasting and brushing away curls with great flurry until I realize that all I have to do is turn my face into it. I can walk that way for a while, head turned to the side like a soldier passing a reviewing stand.

The field begins to fall away, down toward the pond, and the wind softens. I can watch where I am going now. I can look to the side into the woods where we used to keep the horses, in the shade of the pine trees in the heat of the summer. I can find the place where the fence is still in place, bent into deep curves between splintered gray posts that lean at odd angles. I can see my tree, the one whose trunk makes me sit up very straight even as I lower myself to the ground for a good cry.

I have not been here, on this fencerow, in a long time. Nothing and everything has kept me away. Nothing has prevented me from coming. No signs saying, Keep Out! No washed-out lanes or fallen trees or overgrown crops to block the way. Everything has prevented me from coming. People and places calling out, Me! Me! My own inertia.

But I am here now. And it feels, of course, as though I always have been.

I am at the corner. I turn from the fencerow toward the pond. This is the lowest spot of the field. There are still a few stalks of cotton stabbing the sky, end stalks rooted in land too wet for the cotton picker. I break off a stem. Three bolls, white as a Clorox'ed dress shirt, dangle from the sharp brown burs. They are the remains. They are what is left. I walk on.

At the edge of the pond a strip of green sprouts up. Grass.

The promise of spring. I look down at my hand where the stem of cotton hangs upside down.

Remember the grade school puzzles: Which of these is not like the others? I always figured them out. Always. I have always been good at categorization, at locating differences, at putting things into their places.

This time I am not sure. Is the grass out of place? Or is the cotton? On this balmy January Sunday, am I to be amazed that grass has already sprouted or that cotton has managed to survive? Is one braver or stronger than the other? Is it a greater miracle to arrive ahead of schedule or to persevere long after others have given in?

Up the hill now. I can see the top of the sycamore tree in Mama and Daddy's backyard. The equipment shelter comes into view. The grain bins are in sight again. I turn back onto the road and head home.

I remember now why I have to forsake the road sometimes. I can't say how many miles I have walked, but I know exactly how far I have gone. Far enough to remember that coming and going are equally worthy of celebration, that running ahead and lagging behind are both respectful ways of getting somewhere, and that the path you take can always be the one that leads you where you need to go.

FEBRUARY 8, 2015

I want to believe the groundhog.

I am lying on my back, struggling to breathe. The pounding in my head is like that of the pistons in a John Deere 4430, the incessant rhythm interrupted only by spasmodic coughs that sound like a dog with distemper. Blinds pulled low, covers pulled high, I can hear the wind keening across the open fields like the proverbial freight train. From the front porch I hear the sound of two rocking chairs crashing forward in quick succession, and I am startled into wondering whether they have managed to remain on the porch or have been thrown into the overgrown shrubbery.

In the moments when the wind dies down, the sound of wind chimes—normally melodiously soothing—is irritatingly cacophonous, and I question whether I have enough strength to open the door, climb up on something, anything, and take them down from their perch so they will just...shut...up.

It is at this moment that the news at the top of the hour includes the announcement that General Beauregard Lee did not see his shadow and we, or at least those of us in Georgia, can expect an early spring. It is a measure of how badly I feel that I am willing to place my hope for the future in a rodent dressed like a Civil War general.

Having determined, in fact, that I do not have the strength to disarm the wind chimes, I am left with nothing to do but contemplate the silliness, the irrationality, and the ultimate irresponsibility of not just my, but everyone else's, need for a tangible sign that the end of darkness and coldness and isolation is within sight. We are enlightened people. We no longer panic when the sun slides dramatically behind the western horizon. We know it will show up again on the other horizon in just a few hours. And yet, before dawn on Monday morning, there were 11,000 people in Punxsutawney, Pennsylvania, the home of the original prognosticating woodchuck, awaiting the appearance of Punxsutawney Phil. This has been going on since 1887.

I think I make my point. And if not, consider that at least six other communities across the country—including the Yellow River Game Ranch where Gen. Lee lives—produce their own versions of the big reveal on February 2. And at each of these productions, there are not just observers but sponsors and journalists and, in some cases, politicians. Last year Mayor Bill de Blasio of

New York City went to the Staten Island Zoo for their ceremony involving Staten Island Chuck. The rodent of the hour slipped from His Honor's grasp and fell to the ground. It died weeks later of internal injuries, a fact that zoo officials did not make public for months.

What it means is that regardless of how well one knows the eleventh chapter of Hebrews, the evidence of things not seen sometimes needs to be punctuated by a thing seen, the absence of a shadow made obvious by the presence of an eight-pound rodent, with or without historical costume.

Three days later, having responded to antibiotics and the house call of my friend the doctor and his wife the angel, I am once again among the living. I am, to coin a phrase, breathing and walking around. And longing, yearning, aching for spring, encouraged the slightest bit by the fact that the General came outside his burrow just long enough to see absolutely nothing.

FEBRUARY 22, 2015

It has become an annual trip. A pilgrimage. And though we don't remove our shoes or crawl on our knees or touch our foreheads to the ground, we probably should. The spot is that sacred.

There is a tree nearby and an obelisk which serves as a landmark, a way to find that particular spot among the 54 acres of granite slabs thrust into the earth like candles on a birthday cake. We park the car and unfold ourselves out, pulling our coats tight and tucking our chins into our chests. It seems not the least bit odd to say, "Good morning, Margaret," as we approach the gray monument, polished to a mirror shine on the side into which letters and numbers have been carved, sharply and deeply, like her impact on each of us.

Someone points out a woodpecker on a bare branch above

our heads and a discussion ensues as to what kind. Despite the fact that Margaret would not have known the difference—she was more of an inside girl, preferring her nature in the form of botanical prints and pink and yellow chintz—we take his appearance as an omen. In a cemetery you can't help but look for omens.

In a cemetery you also can't help repeating yourself. You comment on the convenience of the stone bench as though you have not seen it every other time you have been there. You note the names on the nearest stones and recite the connections as though they are your own. You read aloud the epitaph and, every single time, murmur, "Just perfect."

Repetition creates ritual, and ritual is really nothing more than remembering. Remembering with the deliberate purpose of not forgetting.

It is time to go. One of us reaches into her pocket and pulls out a penny, places it tenderly on the ledge at the bottom of the stone. She covers it briefly with her gloved hand.

"Why the penny?" someone asks.

It is a story, surprisingly, that the rest of us have not heard: Margaret used to volunteer at her church by driving "old people" to doctors' appointments. (She was in her seventies at the time.) Some of the old people were grateful and gracious, some not so much. One day she was driving one of the sweet ones and the woman, upon being delivered back home, reached for Margaret's hand and slipped her a penny. "Thank you," she said, "for being my friend."

"Every now and then," the penny-placer tells us as we stand with hunched shoulders in the bright winter sunlight, "Margaret and I would send each other pennies." Her voice breaks just a bit as we all look back down at the little circle of copper, the warmth from the hand that placed it there already gone.

We begin to move away. We fold ourselves back into the car and wave at the tombstone as we drive away. We pass two people walking dogs.

I am old enough now to miss a lot of people. Some of them are absent from my life by reason of death, some by geography, some by strange combinations of choice and unavoidable consequence. Not a day goes by that I don't hear a song or see a street sign or get ambushed by an unexpected thought that brings to mind and to heart a voice, a face, a touch of someone gone. Sometimes there are tears. Sometimes there is a soft sigh or a sharp gasp. Often there is a smile. But always, always there is the longing.

I want a pocketful of pennies. I want to hand them out to all the ones who are gone. I want to say, "Thank you for being my friend."

MARCH 8, 2015

This is what I heard. This is what I heard this morning. This is what I heard this morning when I walked outside into sunshine. When I walked outside into air that was warm and slightly cloying. This is what I heard: the songs of at least six different birds rising up gently from the branch like the voice of a mother awakening her sleeping child. And this is what I heard: the drip drip drip of water off the roof onto the curved mouth of the gutter, a message delivered by tom-tom.

This is what I saw. This is what I saw this morning. This is what I saw this morning when I stepped out onto the grass and crossed the yard. When I tilted my head and stared up at the tip top of the sycamore tree where a few scattered seed pods still clung to the branches. This is what I saw: drops of dew clinging to tiny buds as though impervious to the pull of gravity, drops of dew shaped like tears and clear as a prism. And this is what I saw: dandelions, flat and green, leaves splayed out like a first grader's drawing of the sun, along with spindly stems of wild verbena sprouting fingers of purple, rolled tight still, but aching to unfurl.

Every year, it seems, I find myself struggling toward spring, weary and weakened by the short days, the cold nights. Every year I fall toward some invisible finish line, like Philippides bearing the news of the victory at Marathon, not dead, but nearly so. This year, especially, I have been worn down by sympathetic misery for the people in Boston and Buffalo and Syracuse. Watching the videos of cars careening over iced highways and snow plows creating mountains along residential streets, I whisper a prayer of supplication for anyone who is cold and a prayer of thanksgiving that my weather extremes involve gnats and humidity.

So it was that I opened the back door this morning and realized that I did not need a coat—not even a sweater. Opened the back door and felt my eyes narrow against brightness both so foreign I hardly recognized it and so familiar I wanted to rush into its arms. Opened the back door and breathed in air that did not burn my throat.

And this is what I knew. This is what I knew standing in the light, standing in the breeze, standing in the music of the morning: the earth has survived another winter. By doing nothing more than resting and remaining it has defeated the darkness. No orbit was changed. No axis adjusted. No atmosphere altered.

As the realization rolled over me, I walked around the yard to take its pulse. Weeds already sprouting in the herb garden; mint escaping its borders; dead leaves from the oak and sycamore trees choking the iris and day lily stalks. Winter always leaves a trail.

Stopping myself just before I bent down to pull a handful of trespassing green, I realized that there was something else I knew: I knew that I, too, have survived another winter. Somehow. Someway. Through no effort and despite all the complaining.

It is amazing what happens when one does nothing but wait.

I doubt that I will ever be a lover of the dim season. I suspect that I will always face down the cold and dark with belligerence and anger and the smallest amount of whining. But, like Philippides, I will finish. I will see the winter through and I will welcome each spring as though it is the first that has ever been, echoing his final words, "Joy to you, we've won! Joy to you!"

MARCH 22, 2015

The color of this early morning in not-quite spring is liquid lavender, is pearly pink, is slightly silver in the way it glints and glows. The sky and the fields and everything in them are shaded as though tinted by a crayon unwrapped and swiped across the countryside with its long barrel, the sharp tip forgotten. Outlines and details are unimportant to the day as it languorously wakens.

I must be such an irritation, I with my door closing and opening. I with my heels clicking against the cement carport. I with my agitation born of hurry. Morning was not meant to be wasted on such as this, I think as I drive away from the shimmering landscape.

Five minutes, two miles of dirt road, and I see the first headlights. With every mile they increase in number, pinpricks puncturing the softness of morning. I remember the packages of needles my mother used to buy, a sheet of crisp red aluminum foil pierced by twelve needles all placed carefully into their slots. Over time, as Mama used the needles and replaced them, not so precisely, in the foil, it became soft and wrinkled, new holes appearing, connecting to each other, making bigger holes, holes that became slits, then slashes, until it, the red foil card, was something else entirely. That is what the morning sky looks like as car after car after car crests the rise in front of me.

I pay a lot of attention to the night sky. I have wished upon many a star, talked to many a moon. I have tilted my neck and stretched out my arms from roofs and beaches and yards and stared into blue blackness so deep that it swallowed me up completely. I have gasped and sighed and wept and wondered why I cannot simply reach out and grasp the sterling stillness, clutch it in my fist and hold it close.

I have not had such a love affair with morning. I have watched the sun rise over water and fencerows and blinked my eyes at the brilliance, but ours has been a platonic relationship. We are so much alike, morning and I. Busy and eager and...productive. No mystery. No seduction. No allure of the unknown.

Until now. Until this morning. This morning with its whisper of breeze that tugs at my hair and tickles my cheek and turns me, for just a moment, into an ingenue. That makes me want to sit on the steps and stare into the blush that hovers over the treetops, hugging my knees to my chest so that my heart doesn't fall out. That makes me want to drive and drive and drive toward the warm bubble on the horizon, pulled like a magnet toward the one thing I can never reach.

So now the light is overhead. The colors are distinct. Edges have appeared. Day is upon me and I am mooning over morning.

It is reassuring to realize that one can still learn, can still grow, can still change. That after all the living that tends to dull the senses, all the experience that tends to create cynicism, all the birthdays that tend to chronicle fewer and fewer moments of amazement, one can still be caught unawares.

Tonight I'll be staring at that splinter of moon dangling over Sandhill, still enamored of its magic and infatuated by its beauty, but tomorrow morning, without a tad of guilt or a smidgen of remorse, I'll be flirting with the sunrise. When it comes to this astonishing world, I can be gladly polyamorous.

APRIL 5, 2015

Like pieces of a jigsaw puzzle, his shoulder fits into the hollow of my side and the loop of my arm conforms to the back of his neck. Exactly. Perfectly. I have to tilt my chin only slightly to rest it on the blond head, to draw in the scent of little boy. One chair, the two of us.

He has brought me a stack of books, books carefully chosen from the shelves in the guest room. Some were pulled out, opened, and pushed back in with a peremptory, "Too much words." These, the ones about the wombat, the caterpillar, and the goose, apparently have just the right ratio of words to pictures. Who knew?

The first one we will read is *Petunia*, the one about the goose. The plot goes something like this: Petunia finds a book in the meadow, and because she has seen the little boy who lives on the farm taking a book to school and has heard his father say, "He who owns Books and loves them is wise," Petunia anoints herself the barnyard sage and sets about addressing all the other animals' problems. Addressing them, not solving them, for whatever Petunia suggests only makes the situations worse. Eventually Petunia figures out that it takes more than owning a book or carrying it around to make a person, or a goose, wise.

Jackson likes Petunia especially, I think, not because at four years old he understands the message, but because of the voices. I make Petunia sound like a Southern grandma. The horse sounds like Mr. Ed and the cow sounds like Elsie. The dog barks out his every word and the rooster cock-a-doodle-doos his. I love that I can make him laugh. I love that he balls his little hands into fists and draws them up to his face and hunches his shoulders as though trying to contain something combustible.

So here we are, settled in and ready. Jackson lifts the cover and folds it back. I wait for him to turn the first page, but he stops. He is looking at the inscription written on the frontispiece, the inscription written by the mother of the little girl, now a teenager, who gave me *Petunia*. "To the one who has taught me that opening the books is what is most important."

Opening the book. Not owning the book. Not carrying it around. Not showing it off. It is the lesson that Petunia ultimately learns, but only after spreading misinformation and bad advice all over the barnyard and, in the end, nearly blowing up all her friends by mistaking dynamite for candy.

I start reading. I do all the voices. I keep my arm tucked close around this little person who carries some of my very DNA. But I am simultaneously wondering about that inscription. I am asking myself a question. Have I really done that for which my friend gave me credit? Have I really demonstrated to the people I love, all of them, that what we own, what we carry, can never be the measure of what we know? That it is only by letting ourselves be opened, only by allowing our spines to be cracked, our pages turned down, our margins scribbled upon that we become wise? That we learn to distinguish dynamite from candy?

I can't know. Not for sure.

"The end," I say, closing the back cover on Petunia and her newfound wisdom.

"Now this one." Jackson pulls the caterpillar book from the stack and hands it over to me. I can't know, but he does. He trusts me to know what to do with a book.

APRIL 19, 2015

Just past the shed, along what would be a fencerow if there was a fence, the field lies flat and even. Not like a pane of glass, but like a table covered in a cloth smoothed by hands smelling of dish soap and lotion, with vague and uneven undulations that beg to be smoothed. Cut over and harrowed, it holds no sign of what grew there last year or the year before or the decades of years before.

From the front porch another readied field stretches to the stand of pines that borders Jackson Branch Swamp. From the back deck the land rises and falls toward the big pond. From the kitchen window I can see clear to the property line. An unobstructed view in every direction. The landscape is beautifully empty.

This time of year, these days of eager patience, is the target toward which I aim in the darkness and wetness and coldness of winter. This time of year, this trembling interlude, is what holds my feet to this patch of dirt through breathtaking heat. I want to pause the earth in its orbit. Stay, I would command. Remain in this moment, this balmy and pleasant and hopeful moment.

Within days, though, tractors pulling planters will be interrupting the silence, rattling across the flatness creating furrows, inserting seeds. The interlude will be over and the counting will begin. Ten to twelve days for corn to break the surface, for the green spikes to pierce the crusty topsoil like a knife through pound cake. Then ninety to a hundred days to maturity, to fat yellow kernels that push up against each other in long rows. And then fourteen more days before the combine will roll down rows of stalks gone brown and papery to rip the cobs from the stalks, to toss and shuck and shell in an amazing show of mechanization.

Counting. Always counting.

It is one of the first things we are taught. "One, two, three," we recite to our babies and urge them to repeat, applauding madly when they do. We learn new languages and begin with the numbers. Uno, dos, tres. Un, deux, trois. Eins, zwei, drei. And as soon as we learn the cardinals it is but a short leap to the ordinals—first and second and third—because we must be able not only to enumerate and quantify but also to rank. First. Biggest. Longest.

Fastest. Best.

There is, though, another side to counting. We proclaim "That counts" when we wish to convey significance or "That doesn't count" when we wish to deny legitimacy. Neither has anything at all to do with numbers, ordinal or cardinal, but rather with meaning and value. It transforms the objective and impersonal to the subjective and oh so personal. It moves the process of evaluation from the head to the heart.

I have watched forty years of green sprouts twist and turn their way up into daylight and heard forty years of wind whistle through dry stalks. I have smelled forty years of diesel fuel puff black into the blue sky and felt forty years of damp earth on my bare feet after a prayed-for rain. And, though I have never crossed off the boxes on a John Deere calendar tacked to the wall or made a notation in a fat yellow notebook I keep in my shirt pocket, I have counted.

I have counted because I chose to make this place my home. I chose to plant my feet and my heart in this place from which I can see farther than just the pines and the pond and the land line. From this place, I can see the cardinal and the ordinal, the sun and the moon, the past and the future, everything there is to see.

MAY 3, 2015

Sixteen years ago the house looked like a woman without makeup, a Christmas tree without ornaments, a painting without a frame—lovely but plain. So I planted.

Loropetalum and Indian hawthorn and ligustrum and holly. Lots of holly. Compacta holly. Nellie R. holly. Yaupon holly. And, along the eastern wall with four windows that framed the morning sun every day and the rising full moon twelve times a year, burfordi holly. Eighteen burfordi holly.

They arrived in black plastic containers the size of sand buckets and, thrust into holes carefully computed to be exactly the same distance apart, they looked awfully puny. As though plants could have rickets. How they would ever turn into anything that resembled a hedge was beyond me.

As Nature does, though, she stayed on those little holly bushes like a Parris Island drill sergeant. Before I knew it, they had grown together in a long spiky row, a line of fatigue-clad Marines standing at attention and armed with bayonets. And by the next time I took a good look, tiny red berries were poking through the spaces between the stiff curved leaves. That Christmas, I clipped enough to circle some candles and spread down the mantle.

The bushes kept growing, oblivious to waves of drought and over-wet winters. They grew as tall as the brick foundation, as tall as the porch. They made a little house around the heat pump. They stayed green all year long, reminding me that some things do last. I had them trimmed a couple of times, the rogue sprouts and renegade branches surrendering easily to a few quick slices of the chainsaw. Beyond that, though, they did their job in the face of benign neglect.

Neglect, however, is never really benign. Plants and places and people need attention. Eventually the failure to notice, to tend, to make a priority will result in wild overgrowth.

I was sitting in my study the other day, doing my best to pull words from the outer space that is my imagination. I lifted my fingers from the keyboard and pushed my chair away from the desk, turned my head to look out the window. It is what I always do to catch my mental breath, to dust the furniture and sweep the floor of all the thought dust that has collected in my mind.

The flat fields, the far line of pine trees. The loop of the power line cutting across the clouds. Sometimes a wavy V of geese or a there-and-gone-again streak of hawk. I can see through those panes of glass enough of the world to remind me of how small I am, how small my problems are. I can see enough of life to make me want to fling open my arms, dropping all the valueless trinkets, embracing the magic and mystery of all that is.

Only this time I couldn't see anything but shiny green leaves and a thin sliver of sky.

While I'd been otherwise occupied, while I'd been encumbered with much doing, while I'd been benignly neglecting the holly, it had grown so high that it blocked the light. I looked around the room. I hadn't even noticed how dark it was, hadn't noticed that I'd had to turn on the overhead light in the middle of the day.

I went outside to look. All the way down the side of the house, the holly bushes had grown into trees. All four windows were covered with only the head jambs and parts of the very top panes visible. Every single day I had seen that side of the house. Driving home from work, ending a long walk. And I'd never noticed that the light was being driven out. I had adapted to the darkness without even knowing it.

It didn't take long to make the larger application, to realize that I'd probably done the same thing with figurative darkness. Check. Got it. Now on to getting those bushes trimmed.

I started looking for someone to do the job, to prune, cut back—shoot!—cut down, if necessary. I made phone calls, sent emails, asked for referrals. Nobody wanted the job. Nobody.

Clearly, recognizing the darkness was only part of the problem. Most of us know ourselves well enough to see when our anger is out of control or our laziness is interfering with our work, when we've been overeating or drinking, when our spending habits reflect poor stewardship. The hard part is finding the person inside who is willing to stop the spending, the eating, the drinking, who is willing to take control of the anger and put aside the laziness. The hard part is finding somebody to cut down the bushes.

I think I've found somebody. He's coming in a couple of weeks. I hope I can stand it that long.

MAY 17, 2015

It is a fashion rule that has been around so long it is, like a politician, known by its initials: LBD. Little black dress. Every woman must have one. Young or old or in-between. Southerner or Yankee, debutante or farm wife. You can dress it up or dress it down. A well-made LBD in a classic style will last forever. And you will be prepared to accept any invitation.

At last count, I had nine black dresses. Long sleeves, short sleeves, no sleeves. Cotton and jersey and wool. Sheath and shirtwaist. Tonight I am standing in the closet staring at them, hoping one of them will just jump off the hanger and end my agony of decision because, quite frankly, I'm not up to choosing. I simply can't make it matter one bit what I will wear day after tomorrow when I get into the car and drive, yet again, to the funeral of somebody I love.

The last time I saw Denise it was the day before Easter and we were in a backyard flush with azaleas and happy children. She held the newborn baby cousin with the ease of the well practiced, fending off with sweet smiles and gentle coos anyone who ventured close enough to think she might get a turn at snuggling this creature so fresh from heaven. We rolled our eyes in sugar-induced rapture and went back for seconds of the dessert she contributed to the table—a marvelous concoction made of blueberries from the farm she and Dan own just outside town, pineapple from somewhere that didn't matter, and crunchy pecans that may or may not have fallen from Brantley County trees.

An afternoon cloudburst forced us inside for the Easter bonnet contest and, as the rest of us fools paraded through the house sporting our homemade creations and singing "Easter Parade," Denise sat at the dining room table, chin propped in one hand, smiling and laughing quietly at us. I remember it because it was such a familiar sight—Denise as grateful audience in a family with more than its share of performers.

I am lucky, I know, that this last memory is such a sweet one. Being sweet does not, however, make it any easier to accept that it is, nevertheless and notwithstanding, the last. And it doesn't keep me from wishing that somehow I'd known it would be the last because surely, I think, if I had known I would have...what? Hugged harder at goodbye?

I think, though I can't be absolutely sure, that the last thing Denise said to me, said as she released me from the hug that neither of us thought to emphasize, was "Come see us."

And I intended to. I intended to go to the farm and pick blueberries and walk around and talk to the horses and dogs and guinea hens. I would even let myself be bounced over the rutted edges of the fields in an ATV before sitting down in a chair by the pool and listening to Denise and the rest of the Moodys talk about the neighbors' new babies and this year's crop and that last trip down to Steinhatchee, all while the sun melted away behind the pine trees and left our sunburned faces in shadow.

But before I could accept that invitation, I got another one.

So now I am staring at a row of black dresses, clothes that are supposed to outfit me for anything, and realizing that there isn't a little black dress in the world that can prepare a girl for this.

MAY 31, 2015

The clouds that teased rain have drifted away to empty themselves elsewhere, and I am left to do the watering myself. I have planted strategically so that the hose does not have to be dragged all over the yard. I can, for the most part, stand on the deck and reach every thirsty green thing.

The hydrangeas are thriving in the low, shaded spot between the deck and the carport, pale blue heads pushing their way out through the dark leaves on thick stems. Down by the steps the coreopsis is fading as the lantana comes to life, and the Mexican petunias are just beginning to bud. The Russian sage is already tall and gangly, moving in the breeze like teenage boys shuffling their feet on the edge of the dance floor. On the other side in the corner, the rosemary has been cut back and hasn't quite recovered from the shock, but the lemon balm and verbena and mint are happily rushing over and around each other. I can't help pinching a leaf and crushing it between my fingers. The scent is sweet.

The three pots on the deck contain a single bright pink Gerbera daisy, a good crop of basil, and a citronella plant. Eventually, I tell myself, I will find the time to come outside after dark, sit back in the reclining chair, and test the citronella's powers at repelling mosquitoes. Eventually, but not tonight. Tonight I'm just watering.

The dial at the end of the nozzle has somehow been moved to a position between two of the settings. I don't notice and turn on the water expecting a steady stream in one direction. What I get is an erratic shooting and significant drip. It takes only a couple of seconds to adjust the nozzle, but in that time I can't help noticing how many choices I have. Jet. Mist. Flat. Cone. Shower. Angle. Center. Plus something called "2 Vert."

A true gardener, someone like my Grandmama Anderson, could probably tell me which one is best for each of my green things. A true gardener, however, I am not. I settle for center, which shoots forth water at a rate slower than jet but faster than shower.

Watering, I have found, puts me into a rather meditative state. There's nothing for me to do except stand there and hold the nozzle steady while water and gravity do the hard work of reaching the invisible and indispensable roots. So I find myself thinking about those settings—jet and mist and flat, cone and shower and angle—and how, at various times and through various experiences, I've been watered by every single one.

Getting fired from my first job as a lawyer was a jet, a hard fast blast that tore at the ground around my trunk and left me standing in a puddle of mud. The years I spent at Wesleyan were a fine mist, gentle and consistent. The loss of people I've loved were hard angles, leaving me off kilter, and realizing my dream of being an author was a shower, a baptism of satisfaction and joy.

I push the lever that closes the nozzle. By the time I get to the spigot to turn it off, the water—all of it—has soaked into the ground. I hope that I have been that receptive. I hope that I have absorbed the jet and the mist with identical enthusiasm. I hope that I have allowed the angles and the showers to nourish me equally. I hope that with each watering, whatever its force, my roots have dug deeper into the soil.

JUNE 14, 2015

Across the field I could hear it coming, like the rustling of a thousand pages, the whispers of a thousand lovers, the lifting of a thousand wings. The rain moved toward me across the broad, flat field, a row at a time.

I'd been doubtful, when I left the house to walk, based on the general dryness and the dust that rose when a single car passed me, that any significant moisture would materialize. Doubtful that the clouds, the color of pewter and thick like cotton batting, held the rain that the rows of short green stems craved. Doubtful that the sky would yield anything other than disappointment. So I had headed out.

A drop fell on my bare shoulder, another on my cheek. I watched as three tiny pools collected on the open magazine I was holding just steady enough to read. Then three more. The slick stock puckered and the ink smeared. I kept walking as I measured the time between plops. It was, it occurred to me, the exact reverse of staring at the microwave while the popcorn pops, waiting for the rapid-fire explosions to slow.

About halfway up the hill, the pine trees on either side of the row started singing. The wind was sweeping through them like breaths through an oboe, deep notes that somehow float and circle and find resonance in a heartbeat. This was no ruse, no prank. The rain is coming, the trees were telling me. I kept walking.

Eventually, though, I tired of trying to turn pages that had stuck together and were curling at the edges. I tired of fighting the wind that snatched at my hair and tried to stuff it in my mouth. I tired of doubting. I closed the magazine and stuck it under my arm. I made sure that my phone was as deep in my pocket as it could be. I sighed and turned around.

The thing about getting caught in the rain is that once you're wet, once your clothes are stuck to your skin, once the tread on your shoes has filled with mud so that any one step could be the one that sends you sliding to the ground, there really isn't much need to hurry. So I didn't.

I walked slowly, if not carefully, and wondered how I could have so easily presumed that the clouds were empty or, worse, fickle. How I could have been so willing to assume the sky's offer of rain was nothing more than a meteorological bait-and-switch. Why I didn't trust the sky.

Somewhere in my brain lies the place where lives the strange notion that if I want anything too much I am certain not to get it, the strange notion that equates desire with presumption and presumption with unworthiness. It is a notion that resists the words of great teachers and the comfort of great friends. It is an idea that has no support in science or religion, and yet it remains, so that on this day, standing on the front porch and considering the sky, I did not dare admit that I wanted very much for the pewter clouds to relieve themselves over the dry and dusty fields.

The deepest truths, however, lie not in the brain but in the heart. And the truth is that I do trust the sky. I trust it far more than I trust myself. I trust it to know far more than I ever will. The struggle is to remember.

Back at home, I wipe my feet, I change my clothes, I unroll the magazine so that it can dry. On the kitchen table, I spread it open. Open like my hands at Communion, open like the leaves on the short green stems trembling beneath the steady fall of rain, open like a heart that can be trusted and is filled with desire.

JUNE 28, 2015

The first snakeskin of the season appeared about six weeks ago, stretched out in a long line across the concrete of the carport in almost exactly the same spot as the one I found last year, the one I measured and looked up in the Audubon Guide to confirm its nonvenomous nature. Upon spying this new one, I congratulated myself—since there was no one else there to congratulate me—on what amounted to a non-reaction, i.e., "Oh, look. A snakeskin. The skin of a snake. Lying within a few feet of my back door. What a curiosity."

And it was a curiosity, for this reptilian neighbor had been so delicate in his sloughing, had exercised such finesse in his shedding, had demonstrated such expertise in his casting off that the skin was not the least bit scrunched or wrinkled. The very tip of the tail was smooth and round and the head was perfectly shaped, including the eye caps. I bent low to inspect, and it was almost as though he could still see me.

After taking a couple of photos, I had to decide what to do with the hand-me-downs. Last year's snakeskin got folded up and mailed to Aden, budding herpetologist and the owner of a western hognose named William Snakespeare. I didn't think he needed another one. I could take it inside and put it in one of the several bowls sitting around the house containing nests and feathers and acorns and seashells, but it occurred to me that some of the geometric grandeur would be lost if the skin were simply rolled into a coil and left to gather dust. Somewhat reluctantly, I threw it into the trash can.

Over the next few weeks several live, non-disrobing snakes made their appearance. The first was driven from the cool spot under the hydrangea bushes by the spray of the water hose dangling over the deck railings. I watched from distance and height, with interest but dispassion, as he undulated with enviable speed across the carport to the patch of ivy that grows along its outside wall. A few days later the second was, apparently, startled by the vibration of the car pulling in and darted from the same cool spot up the back steps to a tiny spot where the brick foundation and HardiePlank are less than perfectly flush and slithered his way into the crawlspace. This observation was, admittedly, less disinterested and more passionate, but I managed to convince myself that the darkness under my furniture and feet was what the snake wanted, and even if he could find a way through the subfloor, he would choose to remain in an environment more conducive to his survival.

I was, by this time, more than just pleased with my snake response. I was proud. But if there is one thing I remember from all those years of Sunday school, it is that whole business about pride and resultant destruction, a haughty spirit and the inevitable fall. I was, obviously, headed for a fall.

It was still daylight when I got home. I gathered up my purse and briefcase and made sure I'd picked up my phone from the console of the car. I got to the bottom of the steps and stopped. Frozen still. Dead still. Catatonic still. There on the steps was another snakeskin—to be honest, half a snakeskin—hanging out of the secret entry into the crawlspace.

I couldn't tell at first if the shedding had been completed, if there might be, in fact, a snake still inside, still wiggling and squirming and rubbing himself against the other side of the brick trying to get free from the old skin. I couldn't tell if I was standing within inches of something alive or something dead.

It took probably three minutes of absolute stillness to convince me that the creature that had once inhabited the skin was long gone. It took three days before I could make myself get back out there and pull the skin out of the crack. It took three days to figure out what had happened: I'd been perfectly fine with the live snakes that I knew were alive, perfectly fine with the dead skins that I knew were just dead skins. What I had not been perfectly fine with was the uncertainty. Uncertainty had left me paralyzed. It was in the middle place of neither alive nor dead that I found myself powerless.

I wish I could say that I'd never been to the middle place, but the truth is that I have. I've even set up camp a time or two. But it's never been so much fun that I wanted to stay. Sooner or later I always figure out whether the snake/relationship/opportunity has a pulse or that what I'm seeing is just a souvenir of what the snake/relationship/opportunity used to be. Sooner or later, my choice.

JULY 12, 2015

On the Fourth of July, I walk outside and hoist the flag and drive into town to the Farmer's Market, where I buy three fat tomatoes from a man whose accent I can't quite place but whose tent smells fresh and green and whose tomatoes have just the right amount of mottling so that I can tell for certain they have been ripened to that perfect red firmness on the vine. Having found my Holy Grail, I wander around a few more minutes and end up buying a cantaloupe for $3.00 from a little boy who is learning from his father what it means to grow and tend and share, and a package of blueberries that I suspect are going to actually taste like blueberries. I also find a jar of hot sauce for my friend's daddy's birthday.

I leave the Farmer's Market and go to the grocery store, where I buy a loaf of white bread, Sunbeam Old-Fashioned with the little girl in the blue dress on the package, the first loaf of white bread I've bought since the last time I found perfect tomatoes. I stop on the way home to get gas and a Diet Coke at a station where the young man with a broad smile hands me my change and responds to my wish to him for a Happy Fourth with a "Be safe."

And then I drive home and make a tomato sandwich with lots of mayonnaise and lots of salt, and I take it out to the front porch which just the day before was repainted with a shiny latex paint that reflects the sunlight almost like a mirror. I sit down on the top step and, balancing my white china plate on my lap, pick up the sandwich, square and dense, with both hands.

I pause to say the blessing, that thing I've done before every meal from the time I could speak. That thing I did at first because my parents did it and then because I was showing off my memorization skills and then because it was habit and that I do now, today, because I am looking across the yard, then across the road to rows of peanuts trying to gain a foothold before splaying themselves all over each other into long tangled webs and I am reminded of the essential nature of roots. I am doing it today because I am sitting on a porch without splinters and am reminded that even the sturdiest of sanctuaries needs maintenance. And I am doing it today because I am about to eat a perfect tomato sandwich, because the red juice is going to run down my wrist like blood and I will be reminded, strangely, of Communion. The Eucharist. Eucharisteo. To give thanks.

Elsewhere on this Independence Day there are fireworks and concerts, parades and baseball games, and, much to the joy of my little friend Kate Mock, jumping frog contests. There is celebration rowdy and loud and, perhaps, I think, less reflective of the occasion than it should be. And in that thought I am gifted with another reminder: "It is right and good and a joyful thing," we intone in preparation for accepting the bread and wine on Sundays, "always and everywhere to give thanks to you, Father Almighty, creator of heaven and earth."

Always and everywhere. Always—at mealtimes but also during fireworks and concerts. Everywhere—on quiet front porches but also at parades and baseball games and, most especially, during jumping frog contests. Always and everywhere, give thanks for freedom.

Above my head the flag is fluttering in the warm breeze of midday. Red like the tomato. White like the bread. Blue like the sky. I turn my head to take in pine trees and cotton fields, the nearby houses of people I love, my own strong legs. I lift my hands a little higher. "Thank you," I say, "for this."

JULY 26, 2015

I know these colors so well. These pale and luminous colors of sand and sea and sky. These colors that melt and morph into each other and back again with the rise and fall of the tide, the climb of the moon, the set of the sun. These creamy whites and silvery grays. These liquid blues. I could drown in the colors and never stop breathing.

Today the colors are cool. Thin clouds filter out much of the late afternoon sun and I don't have to squint to see them—my nephew Adam and his son Jackson—frolicking in the shallow waves. Father lifts son onto a boogie board and they wait for the next wave. Belly to the board, two small hands clutching the front end, he is held steady by two large hands at the rear.

The wave comes, building and building and building, and just as it breaks, just as the rolling blue water cracks into white foam, the two large hands let go. With the slightest push, the board flies across the water, floating over the froth like a magic carpet. I cannot hear the shrieks of delight, but I can see the head thrown back, the mouth wide open in a grin. The wave dies on the beach and Jackson stumbles to his feet, turns around, and heads back to Adam, waiting in the breaking surf.

The boogie board is a gift from Jackson's grandmother. She has come to visit from the part of the world where sheiks live and magic carpets are said to ride on wind currents, not waves. She does not have to tell me what she sees. I see it, too. The son reflects the father. Hair the color of corn silk just sprouted, eyes the color of the bluebird nesting in my mailbox. I know these colors, too.

This is a place away from time, away from schedules and clocks and artificial rhythms. The grandmother and I have watched Jackson and his little sister Chambless and have not been able to keep ourselves from seeing Adam and his sister Kate. Fearless Chambless is fearless Kate. Thoughtful Jackson is thoughtful Adam. The one who runs for the deep end; the one who eases in from the steps. It is as though there are four children here with us, not two.

It is our last afternoon together. The sun is slipping quickly behind the tops of the live oaks and stucco mansions that lie behind the sand dunes. We move our chairs farther and farther up the beach as the waves inch relentlessly toward our bare feet and wet towels. We are chased by the tide and we are chased by time. One will reverse itself and one never will.

We came to make memories. And we did. We walked in the village and played under the big tree where my friends got married. We had cannonball contests and picked up shells and, thank the Lord, got the babies' mama some barbecue at Southern Soul. We laughed and cuddled and told stories.

And, then, in the midst of coming home, finding leftover sand in the floorboard and tan marks on my shoulders, I realized it works the other way around, too. We make memories, but memories also make us. Remembering the sweet times makes me kinder, the hard times less trusting. Remembering the victories makes me stronger, the losses not so much. Remembering that the sun rose yesterday and the full moon will show up again next month and the tide is going to be high sometime today makes me hopeful and optimistic, despite all the reasons not to be.

Which is why, all evidence to the contrary, I can see myself some summer day with my feet in the sand watching Jackson lift his own son onto a boogie board and push him out into the waves.

AUGUST 9, 2015

The front porch at Sandhill is a room with no walls. I have sat here to watch the sunset blaze with colors from the Crayola 64 box, to watch deer across the way eating their fill of my daddy's peanuts, to listen to the wind chimes call out to someone I cannot see. One night I made room for a long table around which friends gathered to share food and celebrate good news.

Tonight I have come out hoping to see the moon. And tonight, for the second night in a row, I am disappointed to find the liquid circle of yellow obscured by clouds. They are thick and thin, a vast piece of cotton batting stretched out into an irregular thickness by celestial hands.

It is still. The wind chimes hang like weights in a grandfather clock, held in plumb by gravity and humidity, moving not at all. Six empty rocking chairs of slightly different shapes and sizes and states of needing paint sit like sculpture, their long white lines still visible against the falling night.

I am reminded of the old parlor game question: If you could invite anyone, living or dead, to a dinner party, who would you choose? I ask myself, If you could have anyone, living or dead, sitting in these six rocking chairs, tonight, under the thick clouds, in the stickiness of midsummer, who would you choose?

Names and faces flow through my mind like movie credits. They divide themselves, like sheep and goats, without my conscious thought. Most of them, for totally acceptable reasons like preferring air conditioning, end up with the goats. The ones left, the sheep, are huddled together in a small flock. All of them are people I actually know. No celebrities or politicians. Not even Jesus or Gandhi or Mother Teresa. Some of them have died, a few are still alive.

I must narrow them down. There are only six chairs after all. Who do I really want out here with me on this muggy night with no stars and a shrouded moon? Who would want to be out here with me in this room with no walls and a growing number of mosquitoes? Who would be willing to sit in the stillness and let the stillness do all the talking?

I struggle with wondering whether they would all get along, whether anyone would ask who else was going to be there, whether there might need to be assigned seating so that any particular two of them don't end up side by side.

Suddenly, without a hint of breeze, the wind chime tones out six notes. Six single notes. They sound like the beginning of an orchestral overture. I wait for more, but there are no more. Six notes. One for each chair. Through the deepening darkness I can still see their white arms reaching forward, and I can almost see the notes flutter and fall into their singular seats. I feel as though I have been rocking, like a chair, planting my feet to move forward, lifting them to fall away.

The faces are coming into focus. They have, it turns out, invited themselves. They are, in fact, the people who are always here, always on this porch, always in this wall-less room that is my heart.

AUGUST 23, 2015

The three new boards on the deck are the color of honey. They are planed into barefoot smoothness and stand out against the other boards, the ones that are weathered gray and splintered in places despite my best efforts to keep them water-sealed. Even at dusk, when light and depth perception have faded, the new boards are visible, glowing like wizards' wands.

It was the skinny heel of a pair of dress shoes that alerted me to the danger. Piercing the softened wood, the not-quite-stiletto made a puncture wound twice the size of a ten-penny nail and nearly pitched me down the steps. I caught myself and I wondered how in the world this one spot had rotted and rotted so invisibly. I did not know that there were two other boards on their way to disintegration as well.

I called the carpenter. It is what one does when something made of wood is in the need of repair. It is what one does when one recognizes the futility of attempting the repair oneself.

I was not at home the day the carpenter came. I suspect that there was a great deal of noise, much heaving and hoisting and hammering, as the nails gave way and the three decaying planks yielded. Force applied to overcome resistance. All I saw was the end result. New boards. Order restored.

It is Saturday morning. I do not wake to an alarm. I wake to a breeze that is gentle and sunlight that is warm and I decide to have breakfast on the deck. As I sit down in one of the chairs that circle the table, the chairs that have sat on the deck for close to ten years in sun and rain and, a couple of times, a dusting of snow, I feel it sink uncomfortably beneath my weight. I hear cracking and crunching as the pieces of the metal frame fall into rust-colored shards at my feet. Something else has begun wasting away without my notice.

I don't call anyone this time. Repair is not possible; replacement is the only option. Four chairs find their way into the metal waste bin at the recycling center. Four new chairs find their way into the back of the Escape and home to Sandhill.

This has been the summer of necessary maintenance. Porch repaired and repainted. Shrubbery pruned down to nubbins. Dangling closet shelves rehung. And now the deck repaired and the chairs replaced. So much work to keep this place, this house, my home safe and comfortable, a place of solace and consolation. I'd be a fool not to consider the possibility of a message in there somewhere. And, if not a message, then at least a suggestion, a hint, an intimation that maybe this isn't just about the house.

But I am a fool. About many things. I am a very busy fool. Whatever the message, it will have to wait.

I stand with my hands on my hips considering placement. I move the table a little further from the rails. I push the chairs in, pull them out, make sure there is enough room. I step back to get the full effect. It is then that I realize that one of the chairs is straddling, front legs on an old board, back legs on a new.

I don't know if I should laugh or cry or sigh or shake my head. This is no whisper, no slight nudge. This is a pronounce-ment, an edict, the kind of declaration that allows for no ignoring. "You will listen," the house, the deck, the chair are all saying.

And so I stop to hear. Hear the truth that discernment is knowing the difference between what can be repaired and what must be replaced. Hear the truth that necessary maintenance is not just for houses but for relationships and attitudes and dreams. Hear the truth that I will always be standing with one foot in the past and one in the future, straddling departures and arrivals, my arms stretched to embrace both that which is lost and that which remains.

SEPTEMBER 6, 2015

The first time I saw a beautyberry bush, sprouting from the up-side of a ditch not far from Sandhill, I wanted one. Sometime after that, with the help of a friend, I dug one up from another spot along the road and transplanted it to what I thought would be the perfect location in the backyard. It died.

I decided not to take it personally and thereafter took the po-sition that, despite its Art Deco shape and pop art colors, the beautyberry bush was not meant for the tameness of yards. It be-longs in ditches and on fencerows, in the shadow of pine trees and in the path of gopher tortoises. And every year about this time when I am delightfully surprised by the first poke through the summer underbrush of its fuchsia and chartreuse, I am reminded that wildness is precious.

So a few weeks ago when I was pulling grass out of the patch of dirt I call my herb garden, a small square that borders the deck and has turned out to be particularly hospitable to rosemary, sweet mint, peppermint, and lemon balm, I looked twice at what bore a striking resemblance to a beautyberry bush growing under the deck. Looked twice because it's dark under there. Looked twice because I couldn't imagine something that big could have grown there without my noticing it.

It was a couple of feet high and the branches splayed out over about four feet. The leaves, even in the dim light, were clearly and eerily chartreuse, but there were no berries and I convinced myself that this plant was just a weedy cousin of my favorite deciduous shrub.

A few days later I am back and there is no need for convincing; the tight clusters of berries have popped out up and down the skinny branches.

The beautyberry is native to South Georgia and is an important food for two of our iconic wildlife—bobwhite quail, who prefer the berries, and white-tail deer, who tend toward the leaves. It's not going to be hard for the quail to avail themselves of the buffet now spread under the deck. They can tiptoe right through the pennyroyal and nosh away. The deer, however, are going to have to settle for the sawtooth oak acorns that have begun falling at the edge of the driveway. Considering the recent snake activity in the vicinity, there is no way I am crawling under there to dig up a bush that, based on my experience, might not survive transplantation anyway. And since the beautyberry is known to repel mosquitoes, I am thinking that its placement directly under the chair where I like to read and watch the hummingbirds is downright fortuitous.

Squatting among the fading stems of mint and staring into the dimness, I can't help but consider the irony that something I tried so hard to cultivate has appeared on its own, unexpected and undeserved. And maybe, I'm thinking, it is the unexpectedness and the undeservedness that create the beauty, that turn the ordinary into the extraordinary. That it is never the object itself that is lovely, that is precious, that is holy, but my attitude that makes it so, my amazement at its appearance, my astonishment at its arrival. That it is entirely up to me what beauty comes into my life and what beauty remains.

SEPTEMBER 20, 2015

Summer has begun to fade and I want to stop the calendar right here, pause the passage of time for some period that will allow me to wallow in the sharp angle of light, absorb the clearness of the air, drink in and gnaw on the deliciousness of the moment. The turn of the season, summer to autumn, is right now, this minute, and this minute is not long.

In the morning I linger, stand on the deck to stare at the sycamore tree and its leaves, already the green-gold of an old penny; to stare at the sky, empty of everything except birds lifting themselves from their nighttime roosts. They rise with an ease and grace I can't help but envy, a freedom I cannot imagine, into a blueness so flat and even that I find it hard to believe it can contain their three-dimensional selves.

In the evening I amble, take my time down the road and back as I leave my footprints on top of the chevrons embossed into the sand by tractor tires. Cotton blossoms, milky white and cotton candy pink, have folded themselves into prayer hands for the night, and the breeze that rustles through the leaves tickles my arms and makes me wish for sleeves. The sun is already behind the trees. The last smear of color, a bleed of florescent pink, has faded and I am walking as much by faith as by sight.

I can see the house, can make out the white lines of the rocking chairs on the front porch when I hear an animal sound behind me, a cross between a bark and a caw. I search my memory for something to which I can attach the voice. There is nothing. And because there is nothing, into the nothingness springs fright.

I stop. Turn. Look back toward the sound. Make sure that there is distance between us. I can tell that it, whatever it is, is seven, eight rows in. All is still and quiet for a moment. Then the cry again. Coyote? Surely not. They do not venture this far out of Jackson Branch Swamp. Bobcat? Raptor of some kind? Whatever it is, I do not want a close encounter in the low light of near night. I turn back and increase my pace.

There it is again. This time on the other side of the road. It, whatever it is, has crossed the open space of road behind me, clearly disinterested or, possibly, as spooked by my presence as I am by his. Deep breath. Pace still quickened, I cross the yard and climb the steps. There is distance now between me and my uninvited companion, distance enough to sweep away the unwarranted fear, and I can consider what he might have been saying, what his raspy call was meant to announce.

Stepping over the threshold into the warmth of lamplight the translation comes quickly: Fear, sudden and invisible, has a purpose. It pauses your thoughtless progress and makes you think. Forces you to be aware of your surroundings. Demands that you consider what you know and what you don't. Then it pushes you forward. Out of the darkness, familiar though it may be, into light.

I like to think that there is not much of which I am afraid. There are plenty of unavoidable things I would like to ward off as long as possible—the death of people I love, my own infirmity, winter—but the inevitability of each makes fear, I've concluded, a wasteful use of energy and emotion. What I am wondering, after my encounter with what I'm now calling the Invisible Oracle of Twilight, is whether I might be too intrepid, whether I might benefit every now and then from a skirmish with something that makes my heart race, whether I might want to take a few more walks in the dark.

OCTOBER 4, 2015

I missed the eclipse. Through no fault of my own, I would hasten to point out. My view of the moon being covered by the shadow of the sun was itself covered by clouds, thick and bulbous and gunmetal gray. I kept going outside, looking up into the eastern sky, which is, as it turns out, a rather large general area, and while I had a pretty good idea of where the moon was supposed to be—somewhere up and to the right of the grain bins—I never got a single glimpse.

I was disappointed. I am old enough now that when things happen that won't happen again for a period of time to which people refer in something other than numbers—decade, score, century—I stop to wonder whether I will be around for it. (If it's true that it will be another twenty years before the super blood moon coincides with the lunar eclipse, I will be on the other side of the three score and ten birthdays mentioned with equal parts hope and resignation in the Psalms.)

I am also old enough now to recover from disappointments with a fair amount of aplomb. When it became apparent that the thickness was not going to evaporate, that the eerie Jell-O-like tremble of clouds was not soon to dissipate, that no amount of Linus Van Pelt-level sincerity was going to grant me a glimpse of the big red beach ball of a moon, I gave up. Gave up by carrying myself back across the yard on wet feet, avoiding armadillo holes as best I could, and climbing into bed.

Two days later, halfway home from a walk in the damp dusk, I saw the blazing star. One solitary stalk clinging to the cliff edge of the ditch, a spiky iridescent mascara wand of purple, the first of fall. Feeling the need to extend greetings of some sort, I slowed down and turned toward it, only to see not one stem shivering in a breeze so slight I couldn't feel it, but a patch of twenty, thirty, maybe more. So thin and fine were the flowers, like filaments in an incandescent light bulb, that they blurred into a low haze, arcing over the wiregrass and palmetto scrubs like a single-color rainbow.

I felt my chest rise despite the fact that I had not taken a breath, and I realized that my body was filling not with air but with gratitude, a singular sensation combining awe and unworthiness with comfort and peacefulness and, most of all, belonging.

Two days before, the afternoon of the night on which I did not see the eclipse, the blazing star had not been there. Or, if it had been there, it hadn't bloomed. Or, if it had bloomed, it had not beckoned to me. Two days before, when I walked the same road, made the same footprints, I had not seen nor been seen by these extravagant heralds of fall, intent as I was to get home, intent as I was to see the eclipse.

I missed the eclipse and I almost missed the blazing star. But I didn't.

This summer I read a book about a woman who spent a couple of years of her life chasing phenomena—the migration of monarch butterflies in Mexico, bioluminescence in Puerto Rico, the aurora borealis in Sweden, the lightning display of Catatumbo, Venezuela, eating strange foods, sleeping in strange beds (including one made of ice). She was looking to experience for herself the sense of awe that she constantly observed in her young child, his never tiring or tiresome wide-eyed vision of everything he saw.

There is every reason in the world to chase the phenomenal, to seek out the wondrous, to experience creation from as many angles as possible. Every reason in the world to stay up late, get up early, run farther, hike higher to see and hear, taste and touch that which is astounding and extraordinary and remarkable. And part of the seeing and hearing and tasting and touching can be feeling disappointment when what you experience is not what you expected.

But what is just as important, maybe even a little bit more, is understanding that the phenomenal is not limited to what is far away or what occurs only rarely. The phenomenal is everywhere. The phenomenal is here. And now. And no one must miss that.

OCTOBER 18, 2015

As I lay dying—and by dying I mean in the colloquial Southern sense of suffering from a physical malady nowhere close to terminal, but so irritating as to have left one unable to imagine for even a moment the possibility of a world without the present misery—I was able to muster up enough lucidity and self-pity to remember that the day just broken was, in fact, my birthday and that I could not recall ever having been ill on my birthday and that it was, well, patently unfair to be ill on one's birthday.

As I lay dying—and by dying I mean in the existential sense that we are all, every moment and with every breath, dying—for what eventually amounted to nearly an entire week, I let go of the self-pity, recognizing that when you've had as many birthdays as I have, the law of averages is going to catch up with you eventually and you are going to be sick on your birthday and that, as with most things, fairness has absolutely nothing to do with it.

So, as I lay dying, there was plenty of time for more than a few quixotic, fanciful, and/or irrational thoughts about everything from toilet paper to television to tenderness.

Toilet paper: I have always been just a bit angst-ridden over-paying extra for Charmin Ultra-Soft tissue. That angst has now been alleviated. That I still have a nose and that I do not look like W. C. Fields after going through, at last count, nine rolls of Charmin Ultra-Soft—as well as nine packs of pocket tissues that are, let the record show, nowhere nearly as soft as the Charmin—

I will never again question the extra expenditure.

Television: When I finally broke down and got a satellite dish, I removed the extra television from the bedroom. The expense of connecting said second television to the DirecTV account was simply not justifiable, and I can watch only one at a time, right? As I lay dying, I couldn't read because my eyes were constantly watering and so I was limited, for five days, to National Public Radio. During the annual fall fund drive. The toll-free number is seared onto my memory and I have less desire for a gray hoodie that says "Public Radio Nerd" than I would have ever thought possible. I am rethinking that decision about the television.

Tenderness: I am fortunate to have so many friends and such a wonderful family, many of whom called to wish me a happy birthday. I did not answer their calls because they would not have been able to hear me, but I did—many many hours later—find brief solace as I played back the voice mails, the long string of familiar voices wishing me well without knowing that well is exactly what I desired to be. And beyond the birthday greetings, there were the check-ins, the tentative inquiries as to whether I needed anything, the generous offers to come take care of me. A couple of folks offered to drive across the state for that purpose and handled my swift rejections with a sweetness of spirit I might not have managed had I been on the other side of the equation.

It was from those offers that ultimately came the only redeeming moment of the days that I lay dying. My niece Kate was one of those checking in. On Day Two she texted me that she had just spoken to her grandparents/my parents and that they were going to come by. "They don't have to," I told her.

"That's a useless thing to say." I could hear her annoyance in the words on the screen. "And you need to stop teaching people to not try to take care of you when you need it."

I felt as though someone had popped my hand as I reached

for an extra cookie, as though my favorite teacher had given me a bad grade, as though a photo of sick me was now in the dictionary next to the definition of reprimand. I wanted to pout a little.

Except I knew she was right. As much as we talk about extending care and compassion to each other, we resist it being extended to ourselves. Is it pride, or fear, or some other equally dark character trait that prompts us to say, "I'm fine," when we're not? To say, "No, thank you," when what we really want to say is, "Yes, please." To pull away when what we want most of all is to be drawn in, surrounded by, embraced.

We need to work on that. All of us. You. Me. We need to be able to say, "I need your help," and then gracefully accept the help. We need to work on accepting the fact that life isn't fair and sometimes we'll be sick on our birthdays, but that, unless we are hell-bent on being stupid, we don't have to experience it alone.

NOVEMBER 1, 2015

I almost missed October. It is one thing to miss an eclipse, even a full moon, but an entire month? My favorite month? I almost missed it by spending days and days indoors avoiding dust and pollen and all manner of things that inhibit breathing. I almost missed the exquisitely slow sunsets that bleed out over the cotton fields, transforming the exploding bolls into shimmering globes of pink and gold. I almost missed the deliciously cool dusks that slide down the sky like a satin negligee as soon as the last color disappears behind the horizon. I almost missed the first sycamore leaves curling and crisping and the last of the wildflowers bursting forth.

Almost. But not quite. Because Sunday afternoon I could take the quarantine and accompanying lethargy no longer, and, donning a mask that made me look like an extra in a low-budget

Deep South *X-Files*, I set forth. The road was, in fact, dusty and the fine powder of decaying peanut vines seemed to hover over both sides of the road. I didn't care. My wheezing breath inside the mask sounded like Darth Vader. I didn't care. I needed to feel the acute-angle sunshine, see the purple and gold spikes of color, hear the sweet sigh of wind through the broom sedge.

I needed to and I would.

I stopped to take in at least four different shades of purple and stepped over the ditch to snap a photo of yellow asters, catching a tiny stinkbug riding the disk flowers in the center as though they were a mechanical bull. I watched a stand of silvery red grass as big as my front porch shimmer like a ballgown in the breeze and wished I had my Audubon guide to teach me its name. I walked up the first hill, down its other side, and back up to the crossroads where, in the distance, a double rifle crack reminded me that I was not alone in the October afternoon.

Two miles is not far, but it had been weeks since I'd walked them. I could feel the muscles in my back and legs stretch hungrily. Movement is nourishment. Motion is food.

I was tired when I got home. My face was hot and my chest was tight, but I was content. I had felt and seen and heard October.

I am no longer surprised, but I remain astonished by the synchronicity of life's quotidian moments. I am no longer caught off guard, but I am still disconcerted when events over which I have absolutely no control are synced into a sequence of moments within my one single existence. I am not frightened, but I am forever awed when, for example, I spend an afternoon protecting myself from the inhalation of dust and open my prayer book the next morning to find that the reading from the Psalms includes this verse from chapter 103: "For he knows our frame; he remembers that we are dust."

For a second or two, I stood between the choice of laughing

uproariously at the ludicrous coincidence or crying inconsolably at the singular providence. Stuck between the two, I chose the third option—quietness and stillness enough to hear the voice that whispered, "That which would harm you is within you. That which you would avoid in an effort to protect yourself is the source of your humanity. That which takes your breath is the very stuff of which you are made."

I almost missed October. But I didn't. From the dust of creation, the dust of myself, she lured me out into her last days, her fullest days, her days of deepest truth.

NOVEMBER 15, 2015

Some days, days when I know I will be home, days when I will not be driving, I don't wear my contact lenses. This makes absolutely no difference when I am reading a book or making soup or folding laundry. It does, however, make a difference, a rather large difference, when at some point I decide that indoors is not where I want to be.

Once I walked all the way from Sandhill to the paved road, two miles, with my eyes closed. I don't recall exactly what possessed me to embark on that particular adventure, but I do remember it was a warm and pleasant day, and, with memory, instinct, and the occasional brief peek out of the corner of my eye, I made it to the pavement without once stumbling into the ditch or over a rock, a limb, or an animal.

But that was only once. Generally, I keep my eyes open when I walk. And when I walk not wearing my contact lenses it becomes a different kind of adventure. Sort of like *Alice Through the Looking Glass* or a virtual reality video game. Somewhere between slightly disconcerting and downright frightening.

The trees in the distance look like a three-year-old's green and gold finger painting. Unharvested cotton looks like an endless billboard of white polka dots. And what I know is a field of dried and naked peanut vines looks like an unwound bolt of black seersucker. When I am walking without the benefit of my contacts, depth perception vanishes at about fifty yards and the world beyond that point is flat.

Except, of course, that I know it's not. And as I keep walking into that knowledge I experience the truth of it. I keep walking and eventually I get close enough to the trees and the cotton and the peanut field to make out their edges. I keep walking and eventually my eyes focus so that I can detect not just height and width, but depth. I keep walking and I am reassured that what I have always known about trees and cotton and peanut fields has not changed just because my vision is bad.

It occurred to me today, after I got back home and was thinking that it wouldn't have been all that much trouble to have at least put on my glasses before I started out, that life is a lot like walking without your contact lenses. What you see isn't always what is. And what is won't be changed by your inability to see it.

Some days my emotional vision is bad, as near-sighted as my physical vision. It's generally when I've not taken care of myself, not kept up the practices that feed my soul, not been brave enough to say no when I needed to. On those days, things up close—the laundry to be dropped off, the groceries to be bought, the call to be made—are clear, but things in the distance, in that uncertain and scary place called the future, look anything but.

On those days it's important to remember that what might look like a finger painting could well be a tree, and the only way to find out is to keep walking.

NOVEMBER 29, 2015

I long ago learned that I could, if I wanted, waste a significant amount of energy on totally pointless emotion. For example, the frustration that arises all too often within the confined space of an automobile. No amount of huffing and puffing or rolling of the eyes is going to accelerate the vehicle that has pulled out in front of me only to proceed at a speed comparable to that of a bicycle. Nor will it draw the attention of the driver of that vehicle away from his cell phone or her mirror.

Learning something, however, does not always mean that one is capable of putting it into practice at every available opportunity. And so it was that last week, as I was headed toward Athens and a long-awaited visit with friends that would also include a football game, I found myself huffing and puffing and rolling my eyes at the well-nigh unbelievable fact of having traveled only four miles in thirty minutes on what has perennially been the most desolate stretch of the interstate highway system, I-16.

I took the next available exit without a completely clear idea of how to get where I intended to go, but feeling quite certain that, aided by my own good sense of direction and the GPS embedded in my cell phone, I could get there. Within moments of extricating myself from the serpentine string of cars and trucks wending its way west toward Macon, I felt my shoulders relaxing and my jaw unclenching. By the time I pulled into my friends' driveway, I had promised myself that I would never again make that particular trip utilizing the chaotic loops of concrete and steel that encircle and constrain Atlanta. I had found a new way and it was lovely.

Instead of being hypnotized by endless miles of flat gray asphalt, I had been energized by miles of open pasture. I had curved and twisted my way to Snellville along roads with names like Miller Bottom and Rosebud. I had crossed the bridge at Lake Sinclair and watched the water shimmer like rhinestones in the late afternoon sun. I had driven slowly enough to notice the old barns and the country stores along the roadway and the colors of fall in the trees that lined the fencerows.

A couple of days later as I started home, reversing myself down those melodically named roads, I realized that I was eager for the drive. I wanted to see those trees from the other side, the lake in different light. I wanted to feel myself lean into the curves from the opposite direction. I wanted to watch the shadows slip and slide across the pavement markings, morph and melt into the ditches.

I could have made the return trip the old way, via highways with six lanes. I could have gotten claustrophobic and anxious from the swell of traffic racing around me. I could have zoomed and zipped, but instead I moseyed and meandered. I could have followed habit, but I chose not to because this is what I've learned: There is always more than one way to a destination. More than one set of directions that will get you to where you need to be. Clinging tightly to the map you've always followed, stepping deliberately into old footprints, ignoring the invitation to explore, you will still arrive but you will miss the rhinestones dancing on the water. You will not hear the voices of the abandoned barns telling their stories. And you most certainly will not see the semaphores of red and gold leaves flashing out the message that this, yes, this is the way home.

DECEMBER 13, 2015

The sunshine, coming from farther away now, is nevertheless clear and bright. There are geraniums still blooming in the big clay pots on the corners of the dock and there is just a hint of a breeze to ruffle the water. The long weekend, the weekend in which the Escape and I have heralded the Christmas season by drawing a circle encompassing nearly all southeast Georgia, is winding down.

My mind wanders. I remember where I've been and what I've been doing over the last four days. It's Friday night and I'm in Dublin, smiling as Jackson extends his hand to shake Santa's. It's Saturday and I'm in Nahunta, reeling off packing tape to attach plastic poinsettias to an ATV for the Christmas parade. It's Sunday and I'm at Lake Blackshear, being fed stories and attention and homemade chicken potpie. It's Monday and I'm still here.

My shadow is clear and distinct on the flat boards of the dock, but where it falls off into the water it becomes cloudy and dim, barely visible, as though my head has elected to disassociate itself from the rest of me, as though it has seceded from the imperfect union of the corporeal and the cerebral. I have only to back up a few steps to reestablish the single self, but the feeling of disintegration stays with me.

I have left pieces of myself, like lint from a fuzzy sweater or sand from the bottom of a pair of flip-flops, all along the way. A part of me stayed in Dublin in the blue-eyed gaze of a five-year-old. A fragment got caught in the crumpled candy wrappers left behind on the parade route. A shard, a scrap, a sliver will remain here when, in just a few minutes, I pack up and head home.

The highway weaves in and out of towns, crosses roads, passes fields. It is a familiar route. Again, my mind wanders. I find myself thinking of Ebenezer Scrooge. It is Christmas, after all, but it takes a while to realize why the villainous, stingy, self-centered Scrooge has made a cameo appearance in my reverie. I see him, accompanied by the various Ghosts of Christmas, moving between present and past, past and future, and I remember something I've heard, a theory about time, a theory that posits that everything that has ever happened or will ever happen is happening right now.

The quantum physicists of the world probably lay claim to that theory, but it occurs to me that Ebenezer Scrooge may have proven it for them. May have proven that past, present, and future all exist right now, in this moment. May have demonstrated with the power of story that we are never separated from what we have experienced or what we are yet to know. May have given us an explanation for why the past, experienced as memory, and the future, experienced as hope, are as real as what is seen and heard, tasted and touched and smelled. May have offered me a reconciliation of that imperfect union of head and heart, body and soul.

The parts of myself that I thought I'd left behind, I am beginning to see, are both there and here. The parts of myself that I have yet to acquire, I am beginning to sense, are already with me. And the proclamation of "Emmanuel!"—imprinted on cards and hung on banners and sung in hymns—means not just that God is with us but that He always has been and always will be.

When I set out on my journey on Friday I was not yet ready. Two weeks into Advent I was not the least prepared, but I was waiting. Waiting for that moment of numinous beauty and improbable grace that would make it Christmas. I found it. Somewhere on the highway between Vienna and Hawkinsville in the face of Ebenezer Scrooge.

DECEMBER 27, 2015

Many have been the autumn Saturdays that the pop pop pop of shotguns and the yells of "There! There!" and "Over you!" have awakened me from a sound sleep. The field to the east of Sandhill, flat and broad, is the perfect place for a dove shoot, and generations of the men in my family have gathered there with their friends for what is to them the quintessential social occasion.

Rain made the harvest late and hurried this year, and as a result it looked like dove season was going to pass without a single gathering of hunters just outside my back door. This past Saturday was the last possible opportunity. And that last possible opportunity turned out to be the best possible opportunity for my great-nephew Jackson to experience his first shoot.

His daddy took a spot just behind the house at the edge of the branch, close enough to my back door that when it got too cold or noisy or boring, Jackson could simply come inside. And that's what he did after a while—marched himself in, proclaimed that he was cold and thirsty, and announced that he wanted popcorn and *SpongeBob SquarePants*.

I popped the corn, found the Nickelodeon channel, and sat down on the couch to continue a conversation with my cousin who was home for the holidays from South Carolina. "You're talking too loud," Jackson offered. We lowered our voices, but apparently not enough for him to hear SpongeBob and Patrick because, within seconds, he turned and looked at me with the stern expression I suspect he has learned from his father and said, "I'm putting you on the naughty list."

JJ and I lowered our voices even further, and both activities continued to the satisfaction of all participants. And before you could say Krabby Patty, Jackson had warmed up enough that he was ready to rejoin the menfolk, who eventually, one by one, camouflage-clad and rosy-cheeked, made their way to the house to offer their identical, monosyllabic responses to my question of how the shoot had gone. "Good," each of them said.

I suspect that Jackson will have little memory of his first dove shoot. I suspect that he, like his great-grandfather and grandfather and father, will spend so many hours, mornings, afternoons wandering these fields and fencerows that the individual moments will eventually meld into one single tableau, a revolving mural, sort of like the Cyclorama, with scene after scene of men in earth-colored clothing.

I, on the other hand, will remember his first dove shoot. I will remember that it was on the Saturday before Christmas. That I was still trying to get the tree up and the house decorated. That I was fretting a little over the fact that I hadn't done my grocery shopping for Christmas Eve and that I had been less than diligent with my Advent wreath. And I will remember that he told me he was going to put me on the naughty list not because it hurt my feelings, made me feel guilty, or bothered me at all.

I will remember it because a couple of days later I realized the power of that statement. Santa isn't the only one with a naughty list. Each of us has one. And we add people to it every time they disappoint us or fail to live up to our expectations, every time they behave in a way in which we don't approve or make choices that are different from the ones we would make. We put them on the naughty list and withhold the gifts of attention and acceptance. We put them on the naughty list and deny them our respect and appreciation. We label them as "other" and justify it all.

That kind of revelation is especially powerful at Christmas, the holiday centered on the story of a baby born in a barn, whose parents will soon flee an evil government and become refugees.

I don't want to be on the naughty list. But more than that I don't want to be the person making the naughty list. I don't want to be the person keeping track, keeping count, keeping score. I want to be the person standing at the back door and handing out popcorn to anybody who wants to come in out of the cold.

"To survive, you must tell stories."
—Umberto Eco, *The Island of the Day Before*

JANUARY 10, 2016

Like some kind of wizard, I spent the month of December utilizing potion (Jergens Natural Glow self-tanner) and incantation ("I would like a table outside, please") to excellent effect in holding cold weather at bay. But the cold did eventually come, just in time for New Year's and all its frenetic, slightly underwhelming, overly affected examination of human behavior.

I now begrudgingly pull on my overcoat and gloves, wrap a scarf around my neck, and, saying a silent prayer of gratitude that at least there isn't any frost on the windshield, head toward town on the first workday of the new year to begin again. I've no interest in listening to the news or raucous morning music hosts, so in the quiet of the car I am left to watch the scenery. My thoughts wander. I don't believe in coincidence, so I find myself wondering if the arrival of cold weather right at the moment that 2015 magically became 2016 is a sign of something, a portent or harbinger of some kind.

Only a few days in, the year is already marked by sadness of one sort or another. A friend from long ago has died after four separate cancer diagnoses over a period of twenty years. Catastrophic flooding has erased lives and livelihoods from a swathe through the middle of America. A hero has come home to his town, which is also my town, for the last time under a tunnel of American flags, and I have burst into tears every time someone has posted a new photograph of his smiling face on social media.

Is this what is ahead? Is this what there is to anticipate for the next twelve months? Heartache and disappointment and loss? One after another?

Something makes me remember that 2016 is a leap year, an Olympic year, and an election year. Each of them contains a hard "l" sound, what linguists call the alveolar lateral approximant, a complicated phrase that simply describes from where in the mouth the sound comes and how much air is used to make it. It is the sound that gives us the words love and life and lily. Light and lush and laughter. Lovely words. Words that skip and twirl and dance their way out into the world. But it is also the sound that gives us loss and lack and liar. Lame and lust and lazy. Words that shuffle and stumble and trip over cracks in the sidewalk.

A single sound can be both lovely and vile. A single sound can be graceful and clumsy. A single sound can be the source of life and death. Surely, then, a year, even one that begins with heartache and disappointment, has room for more than just that. Surely it can hold a place for dancing, an occasion for laughter, a reason to keep loving. Surely an entire year, made of so many sounds—the sounds of babies sighing in deep sleep, of geese rising in a wild rush of wings, of waves flailing against the shore at high tide—must hold a place for celebration, too.

If I can make myself believe that, if I can make myself listen for the sounds, for the words that make it so, I can pull on my overcoat and gloves, wrap a scarf around my neck, and step bravely and happily out into the cold.

JANUARY 24, 2016

The wind is traveling across the field in gusts, picking up fallen leaves and tossing them around noisily. They rustle behind me like a covey of quail flushed from their hiding place in the broom sedge. Farther down the road, where the pine trees converge like soldiers in formation, the wind gets caught in the highest branches and the rustle is replaced with a rattle. I am always amazed at how full of sound the silence can be.

Nearly to the four-way stop, the crossroads that I've decided is far enough to wander on this cold day, the wind's rustling and rattling is overcome by the sound of machinery, big machinery, the kind with diesel motors. Harvest is long past; the fields are empty. And to ears that know the sound of a John Deere engine, this roar and rumble is clearly not that of a tractor. I top the hill and see the yellow of a backhoe and what appears to be a bulldozer for beginners.

They are in the field behind the abandoned farmhouse where the boys in my high school class used to camp out, and they are clearing the edges of that field right up to the road, right up to the edge where it drops off into the ditch. They are eliminating the honeysuckle and jasmine vines that twisted themselves into knots and made tunnels for the rabbits that occasionally cross the road in front of me. They are knocking down the chinaberry trees, including the one that I use to mark exactly one mile from Sandhill, and they are destroying the blackberry bushes into which I have fearlessly thrust my hands for over forty summers.

I am not pleased. But neither am I angry. It is not my land. I am not its steward. I don't get to decide what stays and goes. I turn and start for home, the sound of the marauding monsters fading a little with each step.

I try to imagine that swathe of landscape without its selvage. I give myself the freedom to envisage the wideness of the vista and think of how many fewer dead branches thrown into the road during rainstorms I will have to get out of my car and pull to the side. I consider how much easier it will be to see deer darting out in front of me if they are not screened by foliage. I decide that it is possible to see the pillaging as something else, as—almost, but not quite—beneficial.

It is probably about this moment that I make the connection between the field and myself, between its edges and my own. Regardless of how well-tended and productive are my fields, how fine and praiseworthy are my crops, I cannot deny that the edges have gotten scraggly, grown over with vines and volunteer corn, turned into dens for snakes and foxes. Left to themselves the edges will inch inward and claim the ground meant for sowing and reaping. Left to themselves the edges will no longer be edges and the field no longer a field.

The rumbling and coughing of the backhoe has faded away, and I have returned to the noisy silence of the wind in the trees. I can hear the voice in my head now, the one whispering, "Vines and viciousness. Jasmine and jealousy. Honeysuckle and helplessness. Edges. All edges." I shiver a little underneath my layers. It might not be from the cold.

I am always amazed at how full of sound the silence can be.

FEBRUARY 7, 2016

Sometimes, when the moon is full, I leave the blinds open and I fall asleep with a laser beam of light cutting through the window and puddling on the floor, blue-silver and shimmering like watered silk. When I wake up, the moon and its brilliance will have floated to the other side of the sky, the other side of the house, and, in the winter at least, my bedroom is dark as a tomb.

So it is that I can't help being startled when my eyes slide open at the sound of the alarm to find not darkness but a not-quite-moonbeam of light angling in the window. It takes only a moment to remember what I've read the day before about the alignment of five planets being visible just before dawn. One of them is trying to get my attention. I jump out of bed, throw on my robe, and run to the front porch.

The computer-generated graphic that I saw indicating where in the sky I should look and where each planet would be in relation to the others included a line of bucolic silhouettes along the horizon—a barn, a horse, a shed, a house, a gazebo, and, in the distance, a sailboat on a body of water of indeterminate size. It bears no resemblance to the horizon toward which I am looking, a straight line of pine trees, their pointy tops blurred in the darkness. It doesn't matter. It takes only a few seconds to find what I'm seeking.

Through my bare feet I feel the bricks that make the steps and the hard straight valleys of mortar that run between them and hold them together. I hear the night-buzz that still hovers in the branch. And, by tilting my chin ever so slightly toward the sky, I see five planets—count them: one, two, three, four, five—five planets arced across the sky like a well-groomed eyebrow. Mercury, Venus, Saturn, Mars, Jupiter. Pulsing like stars, but closer, brighter.

If I count the planet on which I am standing, I am in visual contact with six of the eight currently identified planets in the solar system. Eighty percent of all planetary structures in my celestial zip code are, at this very moment, within the range of my myopic sight. I draw in my breath. Hold it. Let it out slowly.

I expected—as I read about the alignment, as I thought about getting up to see it, as I hurried outside—that I would, in the presence of such vastness, feel small and insignificant. That I would, in considering that Saturn is 746 million miles away, recognize the irrelevance of my quotidian complaints. Instead, I stand in the presence of the ineffable and feel myself being enveloped by it. Like the solar system and the Milky Way beyond that, I am large and expansive.

I am the constellation whose name I do not know floating between Venus and Saturn, and I am the full moon that hovers off Jupiter's shoulder. I am the Indian tree frog everyone thought was extinct until I sang loudly enough to be heard. I am the missing booksellers in Hong Kong, the ones who sell banned books.

I am crying, tears of something deeper than emotion, and I am whispering, something like a prayer. "What do I do with this?" I ask in amazement. "What do I do with this?" I ask in gratitude. "What do I do with this?" I ask in acknowledgment, creature inquiring of creation.

There is the faintest blush of pink on the horizon. In mere moments, the spell will be broken. Only it is no spell. It is not magic or sleight of hand, this cleaving of my heart. This spilling and refilling. It is what one buys when one pays attention. A bargain at any price.

FEBRUARY 21, 2016

It looks like the opening credits of a science-fiction movie. Or a Saturday morning television show from Japan or Scandinavia. Or a more sophisticated version of the time-lapse photography reel-to-reel movies Mrs. Trapnell showed us in fifth grade. It is a large green sphere that could be covered in Astroturf, from which dangles a chenille thread the color of a ripe peach. The thread ends in two frayed knobs that, like little feet, move steadily along a rope the color of young asparagus. That is what it looks like.

But that is not what it is. What it is, says the caption on the video posted to my friend's Facebook page, is "a myosin protein dragging an endorphin along a filament to the inner part of the brain's parietal cortex which creates happiness." She goes on, to make sure apparently that the less scientifically minded among us understand the import: "Happiness. You're looking at happiness."

I am—as I should be, as the person who posted the video intended me to be, as anyone with half a lick of sense would be—amazed. Slack-jawed, pop-eyed, caught-breath amazed. Someone has made an animated image out of information collected from inside a living brain. And before that there was someone who invented the machine that collected that information. And before that there was someone who figured out where the parietal cortex was and what a myosin protein is and what an endorphin does. Someone with equal amounts of abstract intelligence and gee-whiz curiosity was drinking coffee or reading the newspaper or just staring off into space one day and thought, "How would one go about finding happiness?"

So he or she or they set about answering that question with the tools of science, and sometime later he/she/they produced the moving picture I can't stop watching, explaining in visual terms that happiness happens when chemicals get moved from one place to another in my brain. It is as though the sum total of all my emotions is nothing more than an elaborate logistical system located between my ears and behind my eyes and underneath all this curly hair, a fleet of neurological big rigs that pick up and drop off and keep on truckin'. And, despite my initial and ongoing amazement, I am unsure as to whether I am prepared to accept that.

I get the caption-writer's point. I admire her use of the short declarative sentence—"You are looking at happiness"—that startles in its directness and simplicity. But that admiration is accompanied by an instinctual resistance to the idea that anything so fragile and ephemeral, so welcome and longed-for as happiness could be reduced to a formula, an equation, or a recipe.

I have looked at happiness before today. Many times over. I have looked at happiness on the faces of strangers and familiars and in the mirror. I have heard it in the breathless laughter of children playing tag with ocean waves and in the slow easy breathing of a sleeping loved one. I have known it in the oven warmth of summer sun and in the heavy darkness of winter midnight. It is always new, always different, ever frightening in the way that taxiing down a runway is frightening, the way starting a new job is frightening, the way choosing to trust another human being is frightening.

And this is what I know: Happiness is not formulaic. It is

not simply a matter of gathering all the correct ingredients and combining them in the specified order. If I thought for one minute that contentment and satisfaction could be beckoned, forced, or conjured and that I had the power to do the beckoning, the forcing, the conjuring, I wouldn't. I've been gifted with enough happiness and I've watched enough of it slip through my clenched fist, my cupped hand, my open palm to know that forced happiness is never real and real happiness can't be held for ransom.

Myosin proteins and endorphins didn't teach me that. Living did.

MARCH 6, 2016

"Be still and look straight down at your feet," she said. "Look for black and shiny," he said. They are teaching me how to find shark teeth along this quiet stretch of beach on a cool clear day. I am having a hard time.

There are, I soon realize, a couple of reasons for my difficulties. First, it is my tendency to keep my eyes on the ocean, not the beach. I am inclined to walk with my chin tilted up toward the sky at an angle, much like that of the waves. I am generally more interested in what is happening out there, between me and the horizon.

The second difficulty is that when I do lower my head to scan the ground, what I see are sand dollars and moon shells. Or, more accurately, pieces of sand dollars and parts of moon shells. The less-than-perfect, not quite whole, fractured pieces of beauty that litter the sand. They jump out at me like the one unripened tomato in the basket or the face of someone I love in a crowd.

Nevertheless, I am a willing student. I want to find shark teeth. And so I walk on like an old woman—shuffling, barely lifting my feet, head rolled forward from my shoulders, staring down while all around me seagulls call and waves roll.

The few other people on the beach are far behind us now. We have wandered a long way. It is time to turn around and head back. Inside my plastic bag is one perfect olive shell, the broken knobby end of a whelk, a couple of scallops, and two tiny shells I will later identify as Florida augers. There is even a small starfish, so newly washed up on the beach, so recently dead that it is still red, red like brick, red like blood, red like alligator tears.

There are even three or four tiny shark teeth sympathetically donated to my cache by the children in our party, but none of my own finding. I don't count the one I nearly stepped on, the one I picked up only after having been prompted, "Look down at your feet."

I am not disappointed. It has been a lovely day. Sand under my feet, wind in my hair, sun on my face. People I love sharing it all. Failure at becoming a shark tooth finder, failure at becoming something I clearly am not, no longer bothers me.

Though I have no talent for it, golf fascinates me. Unlike any other sport, the singularity of the athlete is on constant display. There is never anyone to blame for mistakes but oneself, no teammate who failed to carry her load, no referee who can be blamed for his bad call. It has two elements, the long game and the short game. In the long game, power and distance are rewarded; in the short game, finesse and accuracy make all the difference. A good golfer can excel at one and be just okay at the other. A great golfer must master both.

I am thinking about that later, when the children have gone to bed and the grown-ups sit in the dim glow of lamplight engaging in what Ursula LeGuin called "the beauty and terror of conversation." We are remembering the past, questioning the future. We are talking of ourselves and how we confront the challenges of life. I hear myself saying, "I play the long game."

And I realize then why it is so hard for me to find shark

teeth, to look down, to direct my attention to the single spot where I stand. It is easy, when you stare long enough at one spot, think long enough about one option, hold long enough to one opinion, to believe that that is all there is. It is easy to get stuck, be disappointed, lose heart when what you see never changes. It is easy to think you are a great golfer when Putt-Putt is all you've ever played.

I am okay with never being good at finding shark teeth. I am good at watching the horizon. I am the girl who can see far down the beach. I am the girl who is patient. My game is the long game.

MARCH 20, 2016

One year it was biscuits. One year it was list-making. The objects of my Lenten fasts have ranged from the concrete and indulgent to the intangible and neurotic. On Ash Wednesday, just hours before my forehead accepted a sooty cross, I decided that this year I would give up expectations.

Confession: the decision was made with more than a little jaw clinching, maybe just a bit of cynicism, and most certainly with the sense of resignation that always accompanies what we now call compassion fatigue. Further confession: the decision may not have been so much made as thrust upon me. Often in the weeks and months leading up to that brisk February evening I'd felt the sting of disappointment, and I no longer had the desire or the strength to carry the weight of frustration.

I walked away from the altar, the sound of my heels echoing off the walls like a chisel on stone, knowing well that I had invited into my life the opportunity to deliberately confront the way I think things ought to be, illuminated and then crushed by the way they really are. I walked away, the sound of the minister's voice already fading, thinking it would not be all that hard. Not nearly as difficult as, say, giving up biscuits. Denying myself a hot handful of buttery bread every single morning had to be tougher than acknowledging the unavoidable truth that people will fail you.

I was right. I refrained from rolling my eyes when the car in front of me turned without signaling. I held my tongue when my restaurant order was wrong. I decided that I didn't absolutely have to have a receipt from the car wash. Piece of cake.

Until last Saturday. Last Saturday I had this party to celebrate the publication of my second book. I planned carefully. I cleaned and decorated and borrowed tables and chairs. Aunt Linda and my new Uncle James filled the tables with more food than could be eaten. There was a table of twelve different cakes. The sky was high and blue, the breeze was light and sweet. The yard at Sandhill was full of people I love. It was perfect.

Except for one thing. I had thought I would have time to visit with all of those people I love, have real conversations and tell them why it was important to me that they were there and a part of the celebration. I had assumed that all my orchestrations would result in flawless execution and those conversations would be organic and unhurried. I had taken for granted that everything would go according to plan. I had expectations.

And some of those expectations were not met. I didn't get to hold my newest little cousin Abby. I didn't get a photo of me and my friends Melissa and Anton who came from Columbus. I didn't get to taste all the cakes.

When everybody had gone home and I was swaddling the leftovers in Saran Wrap, acutely aware of Sandhill's ordinary silence in the aftermath of so much laughter and storytelling, I couldn't help wondering if there was another side to my Lenten fast. I'd been so intent on letting go of what I expected of other people that I'd missed out on my need to let go of what I expected of myself.

If I could ignore the man who didn't signal, if I could scrape the guacamole off my sandwich, if I could scribble down the car wash cost on a napkin, couldn't I just look forward to holding Abby at Easter, smile at the photo someone took of Melissa and Anton with Daddy, eat cake now? Couldn't I be delighted at the things I didn't plan, couldn't have planned, that just happened? Sarah and Aaron, two Midwestern transplants, finding they have mutual friends in Cincinnati, of all places. Little Ella and her parents walking down the dirt road as the sun set. And me standing at the kitchen window looking out over the now empty yard with a heart that is anything but.

It is still a week until Easter. Still time for more expectations to be released. Still time for the fasting that always ends in a feast.

APRIL 3, 2016

It is just after sundown. The yellow moon hovers in the navy blue sky, and beneath it, far beneath it where the sky meets the earth at a seam, a line of bright orange flames simmers. I stand on the front porch and watch a frothy lather of smoke floating off to the north.

I rush inside for the camera, snap a shot, and post it on Facebook. Someone replies with a question as to why the woods are intentionally set on fire. I answer, "It's called a prescribed burn and is done regularly to rid the forest of dead undergrowth. It improves the soil quality and reduces the chance of wildfire." I am a bit smug in my knowledge.

Later, at nearly midnight, I sit on the steps and listen to the faint whisper of dry, dead undergrowth snapping and dissolving in the distance. I hear a tree fall, a gentle collapsing of trunk and bark, the sound like a weak wave sloshing against the shore. A few seconds later, a second one falls, this one with a thud, a heavy slap against the ground, muffled only slightly by the accumulated debris. The darkness has given itself arms and wrapped them around my shoulders. I watch the glow on the horizon and am warmed against the chill. That is the first night.

The moon, still fat and full, appears again. My friends—the ones whose great-grandfather named this place, built a railroad through its heart, and brought the Indians who harvested its treasures and consecrated it with their lives—watch from the edge of the ditch as the new round of fire begins its flank and advance on vines and fallen branches. "Don't want it to jump the road," one of them says to me when I stop, roll down the window, and taste two days' smoke. Ownership requires diligence and attention.

Later, I go out to the porch again. The orange on this end of the woods has died and left a carpet of soft soot unrolled across the acres of pine trees. There is no falling, no crashing.

Only the moon offers light this evening. It dangles in the sky like a drop of mercury caught in its fall from a broken thermometer. There are no arms to surround me this time, and all that remains for my viewing is a leftover haze, thick and gray, obscuring the treetops. That is the second night.

I am late coming home. Ahead on the road I can see multiple sets of headlights, small and low to the ground, ATVs and four-wheelers moving slowly toward me over dry red clay. The light is diffused through thick smoke, also low to the ground, and I realize that something has gone wrong. There is fire where there shouldn't be. I stop to ask what has happened and, in the dimness, a bright white bandage on my friend's arm tells me. The fire has jumped the road. It has ignored the things that were supposed to contain it and spread wildly into a place no one expected it to go.

By the time I get there the blaze is contained, the equipment saved, the injured arm salved if still stinging. I remind my friends to be careful and drive on, forgetting to look for the moon. That is the third night.

Later, it occurs to me that it is also Maundy Thursday. The next day is Good Friday and Sunday is Easter, the third day. The day on which Christians celebrate the resurrection of Jesus, who ignored the things—death, the grave—that were supposed to contain him and whose message spread wildly into places no one would have expected it to go.

I catch my breath. I smile. The best thing about living in such proximity to soil and trees and water and sky is the constant tutorial. Every day the voice of the earth calls out, "Attention, please. There is something going on here." When I am at my best I actually listen.

But sometimes it takes me a while to get it all, to discern the nuance. Mother Nature can be subtle.

A week goes by. The woods are still and the trees that fell across the road in obeisance to the flames have been moved to the side. The smoke has dissipated and the sky over Adabelle is the blue of baby blankets and chambray shirts. The moon, when it rises tonight, will be half of what it was when it watched the fire scuttle beneath it like an army of crabs. I am thinking of the hostas that any day now will knife their way up through the crust of dirt at the back door.

That's when the last bit of mental smoke clears and I suddenly realize that the forest isn't the only thing that needs the occasional prescribed burn. Bad memories and outgrown dreams can turn into tinder. Unrealistic expectations can become kindling. The only way to eliminate them is to set them on fire. Once I do, they will be gone forever.

Deep breath. Am I ready to let them go? Am I ready to see them curling black and brittle and drifting away on currents of heat? I feel a surge of something that could be pyromania. Somebody hand me a match.

APRIL 17, 2016

I was awakened by the lightning. Not the thunder, not the wind chimes whirling dervishly, not the rain slapping against the side of the house. Not the sound of the storm, but the light. Through the thin slits between the slats of the window blinds, into the flat blackness of my bedroom came slashes of white that prized their way through the blue-veined flaps of my eyelids and jerked me away from whatever dream world I had been visiting.

One does not think in those moments; one senses. And the first sensation was that the flashes of lightning looked amazingly like cartoon bolts, jagged and irregular, as though Mighty Mouse could be riding one of them. Or like Harry Potter's scar. Or like the crack in the Liberty Bell. The second sensation, coming not so much on the heels of the first, but concurrently with, was that there would be a migraine.

I was in law school when I had the first one. I didn't know what to call it. A mind-bending drumbeat in my temple that left me huddled in a dark corner of my apartment, wondering not whether a person's head could literally explode but only at what moment it was going to occur. That doesn't happen much anymore, that kind of guerilla attack. I am older and wiser, armed with powerful pharmaceuticals and no longer too stubborn or proud to admit that I am no match for whatever it is that causes my brain to turn on me with the ferocity of the Furies.

The relationship between flashing light and migraines isn't exactly clear. Most scientists agree that migraine sufferers are more sensitive to light in general, so it would make sense that bright light, flashing light, light in a form or intensity outside the norm could be problematic. I know this, but this is not what I was thinking lying there, fully awake, feeling the beginning of a trembling in my head, like picking up the distant rumble of a train through your feet.

What I was thinking was: This is interesting. And: What exactly just happened, neurologically speaking? And: When will I need to get up to take something? And, probably most importantly for a person whose preferred currency is words: How can I describe this?

The lightning continued. I got up and swallowed a pill and eventually went back to sleep, having made what I hoped was a successful preemptive strike. When I woke up again it was morning. All day long tiny spikes and shards of light, like leftover pieces of the lightning, hovered in my peripheral vision. All day long everything I saw trembled just the tiniest bit. All day long I kept thinking, how can I describe this?

It wasn't that day or the next day, but a few days later, still trying to answer the question, that I found myself remembering the lyrics to Leonard Cohen's "Anthem": "Ring the bells that still can ring. Forget your perfect offering. There is a crack in everything. That's how the light gets in." I thought of the lightning again, how it had looked like the crack in the Liberty Bell. And I realized that it wasn't the lightning I'd been trying to describe, it wasn't even the migraine. It was the crack.

I hate migraines. I never want to have another one. But migraines are the ever-present reminder of the cracks. The limitations and imperfections. The failures and regrets. The missed opportunities and bad choices. The things that, one by one, let in the light.

I'll take that. I'll take the pounding drumbeat and the huddling in the corner if it brings illumination. I'll take the attack of the Furies if it gets me the truth. I'll take the struggle if it gets me the light.

MAY 1, 2016

I hated to do it. It hurt my heart. I stood there and stared for the longest time, hand saw held in one gloved grip and hedge trimmer in the other. Rosemary is my favorite. Rosemary is for remembrance. And once my friend James told me that rosemary grows where strong women live, I was hell-bent to make it grow at Sandhill. But it grew too much, too tall, too wide, and now it had just about taken over the entire corner of what I pretentiously call the herb garden.

It was the size of one of those neon pink azaleas that line the course at Augusta National or one of those topiaries at Disney World—if somebody had forgotten to trim it up to look like Mickey or Dumbo or Ariel. It had grown around the corner of the house into the holly hedge and over the concrete edging into what passes for grass at my place. Shoot, it had even overrun the mint, leaving just a few scraggly sprigs fighting for enough sunshine to stay alive.

So there I was, backlit by the morning sunshine like Scarlett on the hills of Tara, muttering something like, "As God is my witness, I'll never let the rosemary grow this wild again."

I advanced into the thicket, discovering immediately that the clippers were useless. Either they were too dull or the life force in the rosemary was too strong. I turned to the hand saw, grabbed a handful of branches, and started hacking. The scent—that sweet yet pungent, sharp yet smooth, musky and at the same time bracing scent—surrounded me and for a moment I stopped. Could I do this? Could I cut away still-live branches, toss them into a big pile where they would dry out and die?

The sun grew brighter. I could feel the hair on my neck grow damp. I muttered as mutantly long branches sprang loose from my grip and slapped me in the face. It is hard work, pruning. I looked down to see blood running from a cut on my arm. One of the newly trimmed branches had gouged me in retaliation. I kept going.

Soon I could reach the hosepipe coiled like a cobra beneath the winter's deposit of dead leaves. I could see a whole patch of new mint that had sprouted defiantly in the rosemary's deep shade. And I could see that the entire bottom third of the massive rosemary bush was nothing more than dead branches, leafless stems, slender twigs that snapped like pretzels.

It took me a minute to absorb the significance. A minute to recognize the contradiction dwelling within my handiwork. It's obvious, in life as in gardening, that eliminating the dead limbs may also require the sacrifice of some of the living. What is not so obvious, but what I couldn't deny standing there in the spring sunshine with sweat and blood running in separate rivulets down my body and toward the ground, is that the dead limbs were so hard to get to, so hard to see because the live ones were providing cover, that the live ones were—by continuing to grow, continuing to produce, continuing to spread their fragrance profligately across the landscape—protecting the dead ones.

Down on my knees, I snapped the limbs off one by one. Felt the roughness of the scaly bark, felt the resistance as my hand pushed down, felt the release as separation came. Over and over. The pile of dead limbs grew.

It is not easy to rid anything—a rosemary bush or oneself—of dead undergrowth. It is not easy to wield or yield to a sharp instrument. First, you must be willing to lose some of what looks good, seems healthy. Then, you must be willing to feel the roughness and the resistance, sometimes over and over. If you can, if you do, and only if you can and do, you will experience the release. Release from the necessity of giving cover to something that would never be able to give anything in return.

MAY 15, 2016

So, I won this raffle. Not the big prize, which was a pickup truck of some uncertain vintage, but one of the smaller prizes, a pair of Ray-Ban sunglasses. The $20 that I invested in my great-nephew's elementary school fundraiser was $20 that I considered a donation, $20 that I never expected to see reappear in my life in any form other than the satisfaction of knowing that I had supported Jackson's school and increased his chances of participating in the pizza party.

I don't remember ever having won a raffle before this one. Contests, door prizes, competitions, and awards, yes, but never a raffle. I was, then, a little bit tickled to get a video text message from Jackson announcing my great fortune.

Just as I had never won a raffle, I had never owned a pair of Ray-Bans. I had never owned a pair of really fine sunglasses of any brand. Because I tend to do things like leave mine at other people's houses or have them slide down my sweaty nose out in the woods somewhere, I generally don't spend a whole lot of money on them. The $10 rack at Walmart is typically good enough for me. I wasn't prepared, then, for the difference that my fun new shades would make in my vision.

It was cloudy and overcast at the t-ball game where Jackson made delivery, but even then I could see that through my neon aqua aviator Ray-Bans the glare was significantly less and the world was significantly clearer. I also noticed that the work required by my eye muscles to keep my eyes open had been significantly reduced. That is, I wasn't squinting. Not at all. It was the next morning, though, in the brilliance of an amazing sunrise, that I was able to detect the true value of my newly acquired eyewear as my unavoidable tendency to draw parallels between the tangible and the intangible took over.

I am all for looking at things straight on. Telling the truth.

Eliminating filters. Abolishing subterfuge. Being honest with ourselves and others. What I realized, though, driving toward town in the early morning brightness, was that, in my sincere and vigorous attempts to find the truth in everything, I had too often done it staring straight into the sunlight. Staring straight into the sunlight and being blinded as a result.

I'd never considered that before: that truth can be blinding. That truth—offered or received, delivered without tenderness or at the wrong time, accepted without question—can leave both the messenger and the recipient in the dark, bumping into walls, tripping over furniture, bruising shins and hearts. That in the moments in which we are forced to tell or hear that which cannot be denied, it may well be essential that we first don some quality sunglasses. Not the cheap kind that blur the edges of trees and fencerows and flowers. Not the flimsy kind that sit cattywampus on your nose. Good ones that eliminate the glare, reduce the shadows, ease the squinting.

Patience and tolerance and curiosity. Humility and hope and compassion. Those are the lenses through which I need to be looking when I tell the truth, when I hear the truth, when the truth steps into my path and blocks my way. They are not cheap, but neither are they flimsy. Like Ray-Bans and Oakleys and Maui Jims, they are well worth the price.

So, I won this raffle. Not the big prize, but the best prize. Excuse me while I go look at the sun.

MAY 29, 2016

On the slope of the hill, just where the field ends and the woods begin, where the ditch on either side of the road deepens, I stopped to listen. I'd been walking into the warm silence of mid-morning, absorbing the stillness and the pulse of soil awaiting seed, when a sudden rush of shrieking and squawking burst from among the pine trees and scrub oaks to my right. I stopped short, just in time to see the mockingbird swoop down toward the ground about six feet ahead of me, followed closely by a pileated woodpecker.

The two birds flew madly back and forth, mockingbird screeching, woodpecker close on his tail, from one side of the road to the other. I didn't dare move. I didn't dare miss a single moment of whatever this encounter signaled. Eventually the mockingbird found cover in the foliage and the woodpecker peeled off like a fighter jet, successful in some aerial maneuver at whose purpose I could only guess.

It is rare to get that close to a pileated woodpecker. Rare to be able to see so clearly the white markings that twine around the neck and down the shoulder like a strand of opera-length pearls. Rare to get such a prolonged look at that glorious red crest.

I am accustomed to the sound of woodpeckers drumming on the trees in the branch behind Sandhill. It is the bass note to the songbirds' springtime chorus. It is the percussion that keeps the beat in early morning and late afternoon. And I am used to straining my neck to get a glimpse of the jaunty red cap in the tops of lightning-shaved trees. This encounter, though, left me a little breathless and I spent the rest of my walk wondering about the feuding neighbors.

About a week later, I was there again, same spot. This time my reverie was broken by a sudden swarm of black and white wings exploding from the woods like fireworks. Four, five, six baby woodpeckers were suddenly swooping and gliding, one following the other, making identical loops and circles in the sky like the ones I used to draw holding a handful of crayons. Across the road, then over my head and back into the woods, then back over my head again to light in a tree for mere seconds before restarting the acrobatic show. Over and over they slid down through the space thick with sunshine and my awe to climb effortlessly, in unison, from one branch to another.

These were, obviously, the babies of the woodpecker I'd seen before, the objects of the instinct that had turned a nurturing mama into a hell-bent kamikaze. Somewhere in the canopy of blue and green that had stretched over my head a week earlier, a nest full of chicks had slept, fiercely defended and oblivious to it all. Poor mockingbird. He probably had no idea.

You don't have to be a mama to know that feeling. You don't even have to be a woman. You must simply recognize inequity and unfairness and then be willing to stand in the gap between the weak and defenseless and the arrogant and powerful. You just have to be willing to say, "That is wrong. I will not ignore it. I will not pretend it isn't happening. I will bring whatever I have and whatever I am to this battle and I will fight."

There was another, not so obvious, point to the morality play I watched being performed on the stage of springtime sky. A point that did not come to me until later. Those babies, those ballerinas in black and red, did not know that they had been in danger. They did not know that the freedom with which they performed their arabesques and grand jetés was expensive. They twirled and spun completely ignorant of everything save the joy of being alive.

I was reminded of a story a friend told me once, a story about a conversation she'd had with her mother as an adult. Her mother was concerned that one of my friend's siblings was about to embark on a relationship with someone who already had children. "It's hard," my friend's mother said. "It was hard for me and your father to raise all of you. We did it and you all turned out okay, but it was hard."

My friend is a wise woman. Both grateful and graceful, she looked at her mother and said, "Thank you for keeping that from us."

And that, because all good sermons have three points, was the third lesson from my encounter with the mama woodpecker and her babies: The fight can never be about being thanked or appreciated or pointed out as being a good fighter. The standing in the gap can never be about being noticed or rewarded. It can only be about showing up, showing up with absolutely everything you have and absolutely nothing less than all that you are.

JUNE 12, 2016

The French Broad River is the second oldest river in the world. Only the Nile is older. I am not certain who decided this and on what basis, but when I stopped in Asheville to see my friend Lee Lee on my way home from a book festival in Virginia, she happened to mention it and she said it with such authority that I assumed she must be right.

I further assumed she was right about it being a good idea for the two of us to go hiking in the North Carolina Arboretum, which isn't far from the river. We started at Bent Creek Park, a stone's throw from the Blue Ridge Parkway, and made our way up and down trails lined with rhododendron and white oak and the occasional sign warning of bear sightings. We forgot about the threat of rain as the gray sky got lost behind the canopy of trees under which we climbed and talked. When we reached the exhibit center I was delighted to discover that the pedometer on my phone had recorded over 6,000 steps.

Inside the center was an exhibition of watercolors by a regional artist, landscapes and still lifes that captured in stunning realism the rhythm of life in the small towns and cities of Appalachia. On the front lawn was a bronze statue of Frederick Law Olmsted, the father of landscape architecture, whose last great project had been the nearby Biltmore Estate and whose design for an arboretum at the estate had been an inspiration for the one through which I'd just hiked.

And then there was the bonsai garden. Begun more than a thousand years ago in China and developed as a part of the Buddhist tradition, bonsai involves keeping plants and trees in a miniaturized state and shaping them into artistic forms. Lee Lee and I walked around staring at the tiny versions of the trees under whose vast shade we'd just been walking a few minutes before, feeling like Gulliver in Lilliput. I half expected to see small people—most likely in Victorian dress and carrying parasols—strolling beneath the limbs that were no thicker than a No. 2 pencil.

In the center of the garden was what Olmsted would probably call a water feature, a stream bed of rocks down which the soft trickle of flowing water would create the perfect ambiance for a meditative stroll through the diminutive forest. Except that there was no water.

I noticed it right away. And before I could formulate the thought that there must be a drought, I saw the sign: "This stream bed is intended to be dry, the only time it carries water is when it rains. With a dry stream the water is suggested. The water must be supplied by your imagination."

I stopped. Stared. Read it again. "The water must be supplied by your imagination."

The words burrowed into my subconscious as Lee Lee and I hiked back down to the creek and said our goodbyes. I left the mountains and headed back to the flatness of the coastal plains. I left the bonsai garden and went back to the farm.

Days later I hadn't been able to stop thinking about the dry stream bed and the far-fetched, yet familiar idea that my imagination could supply the needed water. How many times, I found myself thinking, have I landed in a place so dry, so drought-stricken that it should have been impossible for anything to grow, anything to flourish, anything good to rise from the dusty soil and, yet, somehow it did. How many times have I managed to envision water falling, puddling, soaking into the dirt and coaxing a green blade to the surface. And how many times have I seen that blade pushing and writhing and willing itself to the surface. A single blade that was enough to make me know that more were coming.

I thought of other words. Old, familiar words. "The evidence of things not seen," which is, of course, the description of faith as offered by the writer of Hebrews. And I realized that, for all we say of faith, religious or otherwise, it cannot exist without imagination because they are both built on the always difficult, sometimes scary willingness to see what isn't there.

I don't know when I've been more astonished. Astonished and affirmed and just a little giddy. Imagination, it now seemed, that place where I have lived so much of my life, is orthodoxy. Orthodoxy revealed in a Buddhist garden.

JUNE 26, 2016

At about nine o'clock Monday night I stood in the middle of the front yard and took in the magic. Over my right shoulder the sun was smearing her last flush of pink and orange across the horizon, a long narrow stretch of luminous light kissing the tops of the pine trees. Over my left shoulder the moon, round and gold as a double eagle, was already floating in dark blue sky.

It is an odd sensation, experiencing sunset and moonrise simultaneously. Turn to the right and it is still day; to the left and it is already night. Look straight ahead, across the field where the first green of cotton is struggling to find its way to the surface, and it is neither and both. Right here, in this spot, one is certain to be unsure about things.

Three nights ago a storm came through, brought down a tree that felled a power line. Sandhill lost electricity for about six hours. It was still daylight when the power went out so there was no disorienting dive into darkness. No sudden loss of depth perception. No need for candles or flashlights. But it was hot. The high had been 97 degrees. It would not take long for the house to heat up, so I opened the front and back doors and a wave of cool air rushed in, a train barreling its way through a tunnel.

I went to the front door, sat down on the threshold, pulled my knees up to my chest, and listened to the sounds of the storm—tree limbs rattling, leaves shuffling, wind chimes shaking like a jig doll. I read a couple of magazines, ate the salad I had somehow presciently picked up on my way home, and waited. Waited for the darkness to fall. Waited for the lights to come back on. Waited to be released from my post there on the threshold.

It is an odd word, threshold. Its etymology is questionable, its use infrequent. A noun rarely spoken except in conjunction with the verb to cross. A threshold lies between, neither here nor there, fish nor fowl. A place where the decision is yet to be made, the step yet to be taken, consequences yet to be engaged.

The threshold is also not a comfortable to place to remain for long. My legs were cramped. My back was stiff. I stood up slowly and stretched. It was time to light the candles.

Now, on the night of the full moon summer solstice, comparing the colors of the day star to those of the evening light, I realize that I am standing on yet another threshold, another in-between place. Is it day or night? Am I coming in or going out? Am I holding on or letting go?

I have no idea. That is what the voice in my head says in response to the questions: I have no idea. And as I hear that voice, the breath I've been holding flies off across the yard like a fairy. As I hear that voice—my voice—I suddenly understand that I am brave enough, strong enough, wise enough to stand in the threshold, to stay in the uncomfortable, uncertain place for as long as it takes. For as long as it takes for the day to become night and the night to become day again, for the leaving to become arriving, for the holding on and letting go to become one wide embrace of all that is.

JULY 10, 2016

I have tried for years to feed birds. Hung all manner of feeders from stout branches and metal shepherd's crooks, tried seed mixture blended specially—or so the bag said—for the birds I've seen hanging out at Sandhill, crumbled up stale bread and sprinkled it on the grass in an effort to Hansel-and-Gretel-like show them the way. And, with the exception of hummingbirds, I have failed miserably.

Friends who have been successful in this endeavor have suggested that perhaps the birds around my place don't need supplemental feeding, that they are able to get all they need from the fields and forests. This has never seemed a reasonable explanation to me. Why would the mockingbirds, wrens, sparrows, crows, doves, cardinals, and blue jays that I see and hear with regularity turn down free and easy food?

One person, who knows how much I love wind chimes, told me that the birds might be scared away by the sound. Another supposition I find it hard to fathom as the chimes have never kept the hummingbirds from drinking their fill at the red plastic tubes dangling from the corners of the deck, nor have they deterred the armadillos, raccoons, rabbits, or deer from coming right up to the house to nibble hostas, lilies, mint, or anything else green and tasty.

The long-running frustration does not, however, keep me

from trying again every so often. I empty out the seeds from the last attempt, now moldy and stuck together in strange Lego-like shapes, and refill the feeder with fresh crisp seeds. I am such an optimist.

So that's what I was doing last Saturday when I realized that balanced in the crook of two slender branches just above the branch from which I was attempting to remove the bird feeder was a nest. Smaller than a cereal bowl, slightly larger than a coffee mug, its armature was formed by twigs about as big around as a wooden match. It looked like a new nest, one that would still be holding eggs or maybe even babies.

Even on my tiptoes it was too high to see over the edge. I took my cell phone out of the pocket of my shorts and held it up and over the nest. Click, click, click. Three photos of something.

I lowered my arm, careful not to jostle the nest, and looked to see whether I'd captured anything. There they were—three gape-mouthed fledglings. Their bright yellow beaks pointed toward the sky like traffic cones, their bodies one round heap of downy softness somewhere between brown and gray. Could I be faulted if I allowed myself the fleeting thought that their mother might be pleased to find a full feeder right outside her door?

A couple of days later I was back outside—watering the hydrangeas, pulling weeds, giving in to my baser self and spraying Round-Up in a couple of places where the black mesh stuff just wasn't cutting it. I decided to check on the baby birds. I eased my phone back up over the nest. Click, click, click. Three photos of something.

I lowered my arm and looked at the screen. An empty nest. No sign of birds. And no sign that any food had been taken from the feeder. I don't know which disappointed me more.

Well, actually, I do. Baby birds leave nests. Either they get big enough to fly or they fall victim to a predator. I can't do anything to assist in the former or prevent the latter. But the feeder, the still full feeder, left me feeling let down because it was all about me and my good intentions, about me and my efforts to help. The feeder was all about me and whether I would be successful at feeding the birds.

Except that—and I realized this when I stopped to really think about it—I was successful the minute I filled the feeder and hung it from the branch. My part in the enterprise was simply the offering. The birds' part was the eating.

And the sight of those babies. Oh, those babies! Worth every single uneaten seed.

JULY 24, 2016

It is so hot. So hot that, by 7:30 in morning, the basil on the deck droops like little green flags on a windless day. So hot that, at 7:30 in the evening, it takes less than ten minutes to be damp with sweat and sticky with salt and for gnats to be going after my eyes like children on parade candy.

But this evening brings a break in the stifle. This evening I am standing on the edge of my earth, the place where sea oats and sand separate everything that men and women have made from the thing they have never been able, will never be able to reproduce. I am standing on the beach, the shore, and over my head is a moon so round and full that it could have been die-cut, except it wasn't.

Its light is refracted by flat waves into a troupe of fairies that shimmy and shake across the water into Busby Berkeley choreography. I lift and lower my eyes from one to the other—moon to reflection, reflection to moon—and wonder how I came to be so lucky to be standing right here, right now. I remember how lucky I have been to be here on other nights—watching fireworks up and down the beach on the Fourth of July, dodging driftwood on a long walk in December.

The wind picks up. The waves rise. The fairies kick a little higher, twirl a little faster. The voices down the way drift off as a breeze skips across the sand and tickles my cheeks, picks at the curls around my face like fingers on a harp.

The memories transfigure. I am no longer a grown woman. I am a little girl. I am lying on my stomach, face inches away from a yellow box fan. I close my eyes and fall into the hummmm of the blades slicing the air and shooing the heat away. We are taking turns—my brother Keith, the cousins, and I—sending our voices into the box and hearing them vibrate back out at us, sonorous and deep.

The image blurs and changes. I am in my childhood bedroom. The box fan has been lifted into an open window, turned so that the spinning blades force air out into the darkness and create a current around the house like the one in the river where we learned to swim. It goes round and round and round the house all night long, tumbling through the window, fluttering the curtains that Mama made, kissing my eyelids, and lulling me to sleep.

I open my eyes. I am back on the beach.

It is natural, I suppose, to wonder what makes certain images rise to the surface of consciousness. Maybe it is mere proximity or some sort of sensory reengagement, the smell of salt air or the feel of sand caught between my toes, that makes me remember. That would account for my visions of Roman candles and weathered wood, but what of the whirr of the box fan and the smell of my summer pajamas, all Gain and Clorox? What about this moment, fifty years and a hundred and fifty miles away, would stir them up?

My memory, I have decided, is a cauldron, deep and wide and mysterious; its contents are odd and unpredictable, like eye of newt and salamander tail, driftwood and box fans. Summer is the wizard who heats up the cauldron, sets it to simmering and bubbling, stirs the contents bottom to top.

Boiling over, spilling out to disrupt my present are images—still shots and movies, black and white and Kodachrome—transfigured magically into creatures that engage me in conversation, take me hostage, and demand the only ransom I could ever pay—my total attention. Only when they are sure that I have not forgotten do they leave me alone.

AUGUST 7, 2016

Late in the day, when the light has bloomed lavender and the audible heartbeat of the earth has faded to a quiet drone, when the heat of the day is old and settled, I walk outside to meet the dragonflies.

They are everywhere. Flashing and dipping over the Russian sage, whirling through the lantana, gliding through the balusters and around the posts of the deck. As I walk around the yard they follow me, barnstorming from above and below, twisting and diving like tiny biplanes, intent on eliciting oohs and aahs from their one-person audience.

Their colors change as they angle up and down and over. Black, then blue, then purple. Iridescent flashes that remind me of peacocks and cloisonné and the kind of eye shadow that only models wear.

I don't know much about dragonflies beyond what we learned in the third grade unit on insects—head, thorax, abdomen—but I do know that I remain as fascinated by them as I was before I knew the names of their body parts. There is a memory, faded like an old Polaroid, of standing in Grannie's yard, holding out my arm as a landing strip, waiting for the sticky, prickly dragonfly legs to light on my sticky, sweaty skin.

That arm is soft and round and does not narrow much at the

wrist where it spreads out into a child's hand and five pudgy fingers. The other hand makes a fist and then pulls out the index finger to make a perch, easing it slowly toward the dragonfly who is tentatively rubbing his two front feet together, carefully nudging him onto the finger. He clings now, all eight legs wrapped around the finger, and I walk around the yard watching the light glisten off his wings, fluttering so rapidly they hardly seem to be moving at all.

I am P. T. Barnum. I am Dr. Dolittle. I am the man on *Mutual of Omaha's Wild Kingdom*. I have tamed something wild.

The dragonfly does not stay. Wild things never do. Not for long. He lifts, hovers, and flits off into the deep summer evening. My finger tickles just a little on the spot where he sat.

It is odd, I think as the memory falls back into memory and the present reasserts itself, that I have never seen my younger self, my child self as an explorer. If anyone asked, I would probably have said that, with the exception of Girl Scouting adventures and one week each summer at camp, I spent most of my childhood with my nose in a book, curled up in a corner of my bedroom discovering the world through words rather than experience.

But the memory of the dragonfly is making me rethink that self-portrait. Other images are appearing, breaking the surface like tired swimmers. Here! they call out. Look! they say. See this! they demand. And I do.

I see myself and my brother and the cousins tromping through the woods, sticks in our hands. I see us digging tunnels and splashing in rain-filled ditches. I see us chasing butterflies across the front yard and searching for grasshoppers among the tall grass at the edge of the pond.

I see that I have sold myself short. I have failed, not for the first time, to claim what I am, what I have always been. I am a dragonfly tamer, a memory chaser, a story finder. I am an explorer.

AUGUST 21, 2016

The bride was as lovely as I have ever seen. The groom as serious. The bridesmaids floated down the aisle like mermaids, the groomsmen lumbered like the men they were. Summerall Chapel at the Citadel was majestic, the flags of the fifty states hanging from stone braces along the ceiling in silent reminder of the fact that the Citadel is a military college, a place where boys go to be educated in the ways of war.

I could not place the priest's accent, but his tone was familiar—equal parts congratulation and admonishment, celebration and warning. This is a big and wide and wondrous space into which you are stepping, he seemed to be saying, one about which you know nothing but for which you are fully equipped by virtue of the simple fact that you are standing here.

We witnesses filed down the long aisle back out into the late afternoon sun and waited to watch the bride and groom, the newly married, parade under raised swords and happy cheers into the future.

The next morning I decided to take the backroads, to wend my way home down gravelly highways with lots of stop signs, past all the churches with Bethlehem and Antioch and Macedonia in their names, through hamlets whose only identifying features were boarded-up gas stations and single blinking caution lights. I was well into the journey when I saw the road sign proclaiming that I was but a few miles from Ridgeland.

I'd never been to Ridgeland. Never had a reason to go. But Ridgeland is a place I have always known. It is the first town you come to when you leave Georgia on US Highway 301 North, and it is the place where my parents, nineteen and barely eighteen, having decided that they would forego the church wedding for which my mother's sister had painstakingly made the satin dress with umpteen tiny covered buttons up the back, drove to find a

Justice of the Peace and get married.

I slowed down slower than necessary as I got into town. There was no traffic. I suspect that most everybody was in church. The downtown buildings were flat-faced and close to the side-walk, many of them empty. A railroad track cut across 301 at a perfect 90-degree angle, but I suspected that it rattles infrequently these days.

I saw a lot of abandoned motels and truck stops, broken windows and rusted canopies. There really was little worth noting about Ridgeland beyond a satellite campus of the University of South Carolina that boasts a few new buildings and the confiscation and renovation of a handful of old.

Little to recommend this town, like so many that have been left behind by the people racing up and down the interstate highways, except for that one small thing.

I tried to imagine them on that Friday afternoon—her tiny waist, his black hair. I wondered what they talked about as they drove. I wondered which building had held the JP's office and if it was still there.

When people ask me where I'm from, I always know what to tell them. I was born here. I have lived here always. But that Sunday morning on the way home from a wedding that could not have been any more different from the one in which my parents took their own steps into that big and wide and wondrous space, I realized that while here is where I am from, it is not where my story began.

Not in the beginning. Not once upon a time. My story started when two teenagers stood in front of a common civil servant and, in response to his particular version of will you, said they would.

And they did. They still do.

SEPTEMBER 4, 2016

Birds, it would appear, read the newspaper. Or perhaps it is just
the birds who live at Sandhill. Only days after I wrote of my failure to attract anything to my bird feeders other than aflatoxin, the
birdfeeder dangling from the chinaberry tree was empty.

Amazed and hesitantly excited, I refilled it and a couple of
days later it was empty again. I bought a second bird feeder, hung
it on a higher limb on the other side of the tree, and filled it. The
next time I checked they were both empty. I bought a bigger bag
of songbird mix.

But I didn't see any birds. Nobody balancing prissily on the
edge of the feeder, nobody gliding through the branches for a
nibble or a nosh. Nobody pausing at the end of the meal for a
brief nod of acknowledgment to the provisioner.

Then one day as I struggled to simultaneously still the
springy branch, keep the leaves out of my eyes, slide the top of the
feeder up the string, and avoid spilling the birdseed, I saw out of
the corner of my eye a bird. Less than an arm's length away,
perched on a branch no bigger around than a wooden spoon, staring straight at me. The same pale chartreuse color as the berries
on the tree. A head topped with a downy tuft of feathers like a
mohawk.

Just a few leaves separated us. I wanted to reach out, to touch
the feathers that looked like velveteen, to stroke the tiny head that
tilted up so regally. But at the same time I did not want to break
the moment. We stood there, the two of us. Staring. And breathing.

It was I who eventually broke the spell by remembering
something or other that remained undone on the list of chores. I
finished filling the feeder and left the bird to its supper. Back inside the house I went straight to the Audubon book and gasped
out loud when I recognized my friend in the glossy photograph.

Female cardinal. Of course. She looked exactly like the flashy red male cardinal, right down to the tuft on her head, but I'd failed to recognize her because, well, she wasn't flashy and red. She was subtle and green, the color of her surroundings. She didn't draw attention to herself. I'd seen her only because I'd gotten so close and she'd been so still.

It's been a long time since I was a girl. A long time since it mattered what *Glamour* and *Seventeen* said about how I should look. A long time since I slept in pink rollers the size of orange juice cans trying to straighten my hair. A long time since I refused to smile in pictures because I was self-conscious of the space between my two front teeth. A long time since I thought I needed to be flashy and red.

Flashy and red is beautiful. Flashy and red is reassuring when it shows up on a gray afternoon in winter. It's inspiring when it streaks across a pale blue sky on an early spring morning. But flashy and red can be dangerous, too. It makes the bird more vulnerable, more difficult to hide from predators. And the flashy and red has never let me get close enough to stare into its eyes. Close enough to share a breath. There is a price to pay for being flashy and red.

SEPTEMBER 18, 2016

It's not that I don't pay attention to the weather. I do. I pay remarkably close attention to the weather. At least my body does.

When the barometric pressure drops, the headaches come. When the humidity rises, the hair expands. As soon as the flowers and trees and grasses begin to bud and shoot their pollen out into the air like invisible fireworks, the breath becomes labored. And in the right combination of cold and wet, the right knee reminds me of green grass and white lines and speeding soccer balls and the feeling of invincibility.

No, it's not that I don't pay attention to the weather. It's just that I don't pay attention to the weather forecast, an aversion that I suspect comes from all those years living in a house with a farmer. A house where conversation about the weather wasn't something in which you engaged to pass the time and fill the spaces, but something that surrounded you, lingered on your skin, left you more often than not anxious and tender. A house where unseasonable freeze and wind chill factor, serious drought and record high were not vocabulary words but dangerous interlopers, evil marauders, malevolent trespassers.

Weather forecasts, it didn't take me long to learn, could narrow my father's eyes, furrow his brow, hunch his shoulders. Weather forecasts could make him quieter than usual, send him out into the middle of the field, alone, to walk and think and pray. Weather forecasts offered information that might or might not be correct and about which I could do absolutely nothing.

So I stopped paying attention. And the storm that blew up Sunday night, the storm that Grannie would call a badstorm, a one-word moniker carrying the connotation of imminent destruction and danger, caught me completely off guard.

Rain earlier in the day had come and gone, leaving the road still walkable. Dave, a stray dog my great-nephew Jackson named, and I had left footprints in the damp dirt and breathed cooler air. We'd noticed that the cotton seemed to be standing a little straighter and the grass seemed to be a little greener. We'd hardly broken a sweat. There was nothing to indicate that the evening would be anything other than quiet and calm. Nothing except, apparently, a severe weather warning or some such thing that had been issued by the National Weather Service or some such agency.

I sat on the couch and listened to the wind grow louder and wilder. It rattled the window screens and keened through the chimney like a banshee. The rain flew across the yard in near-horizontal sheets, hard wet arrows puncturing the ground and chopping at the roots of anything growing. There hadn't been time to turn down the rocking chairs, and I listened for the sound of one or more being thrown into the shrubs.

And then the power went out.

Three hours in the dark can leave a person with plenty of time to consider things. Like whether it makes any difference if you know that a storm is headed your way.

In this case it probably wouldn't have. Other than securing the rocking chairs, there's not much I would have done if I'd been watching television and recognized in that ubiquitous floating line of information at the bottom of the screen the announcement that included words that had something to do with me.

On the other hand, there are different kinds of storms and different kinds of warnings, different ways of forecasting torrential emotional rains or issuing psychological travel advisories. In those situations, it is easy to surmise—lying in the dark, listening to the wind screeching around the corners of the house and giving it a scary face—that advance notice would be a good thing. It is also easy to conclude that staying inside, staying at home, staying safe is always the better choice.

I have, though, been caught without an umbrella enough times to know that the storm always passes. I have dragged my dripping self up onto the porch frequently enough to understand that the wettest things eventually dry. I have felt rain pelt my face, sometimes mixing with my tears, often enough to learn to appreciate the fresh baptism as a reminder that I am alive.

OCTOBER 2, 2016

I have taken up the habit of walking a prescribed path along the edges of the yard. This walking is different from the other kinds of walking I do—the brisk striding to the highway and back that increases my heart rate and makes me feel that I'm doing at least a little something toward maintaining my good health; the slow and purposeless ambling through the woods looking for nothing in particular but hoping to stumble upon something astonishing.

This walking, this perimeter walking, is not slow or fast. It is both purposeful and purposeless. It is a moment in the day in which I reestablish my equilibrium, recalibrate my settings, refocus my attention on the distinction between the urgent and the important.

I am accompanied on these walks by a rosary, a gift from my friend Becky, a souvenir from her trip to Israel. I am not Catholic, and my knowledge of how a rosary is generally used is limited to what I have gleaned from novels by people like Flannery O'Connor and conversations with Catholic friends. Armed with that admittedly limited knowledge, I have developed my own way of using the rosary to draw myself toward all that is sacred.

Sometimes, as I walk and the beads slide through my fingers like silk, each one represents a moment of gratitude from the day I've just lived. Other times, when the soft flesh of my thumb and forefinger are dented by my tight grip on each one, the beads represent the hurts and sorrows and unfulfilled dreams of people I know and love, the bruises and lacerations of my own heart.

Of late I have been accompanied on these meditative strolls by Dave, the stray who has not yet decided if he will stay. He is still a puppy and is fascinated by anything that flutters, rattles, or dangles. Thus, I should not have been surprised the other afternoon when he scampered up behind me, tongue lolling out of one side of his mouth, and suddenly sprang toward the hand clutching the rosary. He managed to get his teeth around the chain, breaking one of the tiny metal links that thread the beads into one long strand of supplications.

It was his first mistake. And because he is not my first dog, I am comfortable in acknowledging that, should he decide to stay, it won't be his last. So I picked up the half-rosary that lay in the edge of the field road and we kept walking.

I have neither the tools nor the eyesight to properly repair something that small. I, therefore, resorted to fishing line—threaded the 40-pound test through two neighboring links and tied it off with knots like the ones Mama taught me to use when hemming a dress. Put it back together with the best of what I had.

Before Dave broke my rosary, I was a little careless with it. I held it nonchalantly, loosely, in one hand. I let it swing back and forth, losing track sometimes of where I was in my journey through the beaded labyrinth, depending on the fact that the trek is always a loop and either way will take me back to the beginning.

Now, I no longer let it dangle carelessly in rhythm with my stride. I exercise greater care. I hold it with two hands, its beads and links sifting back and forth between them like an elegant Slinky. And when my fingers reach the spot where two beads are held together by a piece of knotted fishing line, I am prompted to regard fragility and adaptability and forgiveness as the graces they are, to remember that all things are sacred, to rely on the truth that all paths eventually lead home.

OCTOBER 16, 2016

The water is hot. It is rushing through the faucet, collecting in the sink. Bubbles that smell of green things, living things, rise like yeast. I hold my hands under the water for a moment, watch my knuckles turn red. It is dark outside the kitchen window, but inside, inside my house, it is light, miraculously light.

I am cleaning the candleholders. The bronze ones that were a housewarming gift for my very first grown-up place. The clear acrylic cubes I bought in Chattanooga as a memento of a girls' weekend. The lead crystal ones that belong to Mama who loaned them to me and who never asked for them back. I am cleaning them of the wax that dripped and hardened and caked over the four nights during which they got to be more than just bit players in an attractive table display. Four nights during which they were the only thing that stood between me and the abyss, darkness that fell with the thud of a guillotine at 10:23 p.m. on Friday.

The hurricane was relatively kind to Adabelle. Other than the string of pine trees that fell like dominoes over the power lines, stranding all of us without lights and cable and internet and well water, there was little real damage. The ancient oak tree in my parents' front yard, already crippled by two previous storms, lost yet another chunk of itself, taking out a part of their fence but graciously falling in the road rather than into their bedroom. The chinaberry tree in my backyard that had of late become the feeding station for so many birds was halfway uprooted and left dangling. A few more pine trees in the woods behind my brother's and my neighbors' houses snapped in two—that's all.

I did not have any trees fall through my roof or crush my car. I did not have water rise up into my house like the tide. I did not—I can hardly form the words—have someone I love stolen from me by the violent, indiscriminate wind and rain. I just lost power.

Yes, it was for ninety-three hours. Yes, it meant that I had to drive twenty miles to get something cold to drink. Yes, I had to put on makeup in the bathroom at the office. But that? That's inconvenience. That's all.

Which is why it's a little embarrassing to admit that by day five, when I'd grown tired of drive-by showers and my favorite takeout, when I had to stop to remember what day it was, when I was about ready to just let the cell phone die rather than sit in my car for one more minute waiting for it to charge, I got a little pouty, a little impatient, a little impertinent.

I was, like everyone else, longing for normal. I wanted to be able to do something, anything, without thinking and planning and strategizing. I wanted to be able to look at a clock and check the time, to find the dog snacks in the pantry without knocking something else off the shelf, to put in my contacts. I wanted to be able to flush the toilet, for heaven's sake!

Did I really need to feel guilty about that? Is it wrong to desire comfort? Can't we prefer light over dark without being made to feel as though we have failed the test of human toughness? No. No. And yes.

Hardship is not a contest. Pain is not an endurance test. Nobody leaves here unscarred. Nobody gets a perfect score. Hurricane Matthew—just like every hurricane, tornado, drought, war, terroristic attack, and automobile accident that came before or will come after—was just one more challenge, one more chance to do the best we can.

And the best we can is, of course, exactly enough.

OCTOBER 30, 2016

Within the arms of the tree lost to the hurricane I found a nest. Deep and empty like a soup bowl slurped clean, it was cradled between two branches. In wind strong enough to topple the tree, it had somehow remained whole.

Both the architecture and the construction were solid, and the removal of the avian residence from its perch was difficult. The finesse with which the twigs and leaves and other bits of natural ephemera had been woven together was obvious at first glance, and I knew that one ill-advised tug could send the entire structure falling to the ground and disintegrating into a dusty pile of yard waste.

Lift. Pull. Twist. Turn. I maneuvered the nest while doing my best to avoid swallowing a dangling chinaberry or putting my eye out with a protruding broken limb. Eventually it came loose and I lowered my arms, now burning from having been held above my head for so long, to see that the nest was much bigger than I'd first thought.

All the nests in my house—and there are more than a couple—are about the size of a large grapefruit, like the ones the relatives from Florida used to bring in the red string bags with the graphic labels. This one, the one that survived the hurricane, is more the size of a head of iceberg lettuce—not the ones in the grocery store now but the big ones from the seventies when we first started eating salad and iceberg was the only kind of lettuce and French, Thousand Island, and Italian were the only dressings. This nest was built, it appears, by a couple with aspirations.

I took it inside and, with so many other post-hurricane chores to address, set the nest down in the bowl in the middle of the dining room table, the pastel-glazed bowl I bought at the university ceramics sale one Christmas. It generally holds fruit—a dozen apples or oranges—but it was empty and handy and that's where the nest landed, its outer twigs catching on the rim of the bowl so that it hung like a double boiler.

That was nearly three weeks ago. I've walked past that nest in that bowl on that table at least three hundred times. Heading out to work in the morning, coming in at night. From the couch watching the baseball playoffs to the refrigerator for something to drink and back again. To the laundry room to load the washer, to empty the washer, to load the dryer, to empty the dryer. Back and forth and back and forth.

And this is the thing: I've seen the nest—had the image register on my retina and travel to my brain for identification—every single time. But not once have I stopped and looked. Not once have I slowed down to touch the tiny leaf stems and curly root hairs that were woven together to make the lining soft enough to incubate eggs. Not once have I paused to note how many different shades of brown and gray it would take to reproduce that nest on canvas. Not once have I broken stride and acknowledged the magic and the mystery surrounding the fact that a bird with only a beak and two clawed feet as tools and debris as materials, a bird weighing less than two ounces, managed to engineer and construct something that withstood a hurricane.

This is a sin. To him, or her, who knows to do good—who knows to pay attention and be amazed, who knows to be grateful for the miraculous, who knows to take the time to watch the world unfold—and does not do it, to him, to her, to all of them everywhere, this is a sin.

On the front porch, in morning light turned golden by the October sun, I pause to listen to leaves on the holly trees rattle like a dancing skeleton and dew heavy as rain drip from the roof onto the brick steps with flat splats. I look across the road to see the white polka dots of cotton bolls and the narrow green stripes of pine trees rolled out like the fabric of an Easter dress. I feel the breeze and taste the air. This is my repentance.

After the earthquake Elijah heard a still, small voice. After the hurricane I saw a nest.

NOVEMBER 13, 2016

The morning after the presidential election breaks still and gentle. The colors of the landscape—pale gray, faded blue, soft green—make me think of cashmere sweaters. There is no breeze worth noting. The flag that proclaims "Welcome Friends" hangs straight and limp from the flagpole and the wind chimes ring out only the infrequent single note.

Breathing in the smell of just-cut grass, I realize for the first time that election day and All Saints' Sunday are in the same week. I cannot imagine that this is a coincidence, that the founding fathers did not in some way recognize it and find some significance in the juxtaposition of the two events. Perhaps someone among them considered that the great experiment, which would remain a great experiment even 229 years later, could use an assist from the great cloud of witnesses referenced by Saint Paul.

On Sunday, as is usual, the pastor reminded us that it is not only those who have died who are considered by the church to be saints, but all of us. All of us saints. And so, with that thought in mind, I stand on the front porch of Sandhill, gaze out across the cotton fields still to be harvested, and try to think of myself that way, as Saint Kathy. Try to decide how I should walk into the world on a day in which, in the words of one of my young friends, "Half of America thinks the apocalypse is coming and the other half thinks the savior has arrived already."

In the distance I hear a diesel engine. Across the way I see a tree has fallen, damaged most likely in the hurricane and, finally, after a month of struggle, overcome by gravity. On my face and my arms I can feel the dampness of not-yet-evaporated dew. I see and hear and feel and it is all beautiful, all overwhelmingly beautiful.

I have not forgotten about Omran Daqneesh, the little boy in the Syrian ambulance. I have not forgotten about the tragedies in Charleston and Orlando and Dallas. I have not forgotten the children whose faces I see every day, the ones who live in poverty, the ones who struggle with mental health issues, the ones whose families are fractured.

The late Irish poet John O'Donohue said that beauty is "that in the presence of which we feel more alive." If he is right—and I believe he is—then there is beauty in the tear-streaked face of five-year-old Omran. There is beauty in the passion and dignity of the mourners of tragedies. There is beauty in the suffering of those whose voices have not yet been heard. There is beauty because in their presence I am more alive.

And I realize that that is how I walk into this day. That is the Gospel of Saint Kathy, the good news that I am called to share—the good news that beauty still exists and we will find it in each other, not just in our similarities but in our differences. That beauty still exists, and we will find it when we listen to each other's stories with interest and patience. That beauty still exists, and kindness is still possible and disagreement doesn't have to be polarizing. And in the embrace of beauty we can change the world.

That is how I will walk into this day. And every day. And all the saints said, "Amen."

NOVEMBER 27, 2016

The skin of the onion, the color of varnished oak, rustles softly beneath my fingers, cracks and falls away from the shiny white layers that hold each other tightly. I chop it into tiny squares of moist piquancy and then make room on the cutting board for the celery, a green that is its own color. I turn the long stalks into a stack of half-moons, satellites for a hundred miniature planets.

The seeds of the bell pepper stick to the knife, my fingers, whatever they touch. Their strange adhesive and the pepper's uneven contours make it difficult to produce a uniform shape. The heap of hunter and kelly and emerald green grows slowly.

For a long time, longer than any self-respecting Southern woman should have, I got by without cooking. Lean Cuisine and anyplace with a drive-through window were my primary sources of nutrition. I was known to say that a good day was one in which three different fast food bags made their way into the foot of my car.

When friends or colleagues asked, "What are you taking to Thanksgiving?" I replied, "The centerpiece and my sparkling personality." Grannie was still alive then. She, Mama, and my flock of aunts did all the heavy lifting required to produce the holiday meal that always brought to mind the old English description of the dining table as a groaning board, heavy with more than enough food for the extended family that gathered at the little house on South College Street and, later when the number had grown to fifty or more, at the pond house on the farm.

That large and loud and, at times, overwhelming gathering eventually dispelled, leaving the children of my grandparents and their offspring to forge their own holiday observances. It is no longer enough for me to show up with a vase of wildflowers and a few funny stories. I have, in fact, assumed responsibility for Thanksgiving for my branch of the family tree, and it is as a result of that assumption that I find myself in the kitchen on this night creating mounds of diced vegetables.

I am alone, but the sounds and smells, the sensations of warmth and intimacy from those other Thanksgivings surround me as I begin the preparations to feed those who will sit around the table at Sandhill this holiday. It is quiet and still except for the rhythmic shush of the knife coming down on vegetable flesh, but I can hear the aluminum foil peeling back from Aunt Doris's congealed salad and the clang of the pot lid as Debbie peeks in at Mama's creamed corn. I can see the row of desserts lined up across the top of the washer and dryer in the corner—sour cream pound cake with cream cheese icing, pecan pie, sweet potato pie, coconut cake.

It is all as real as the reflection of my face in my kitchen window, the face of the woman who was the girl who tasted the saltiness of the ham she pinched from the edge of the platter before the blessing was said. The girl who felt the sun in her eyes as she stood in the backyard watching her father and his brothers play pitch penny. The girl who smelled vanilla extract in the heat from the open oven door.

Beneath my hands the chopping is finished. Still left is the thawing and draining and boiling and baking. The melting and mixing and roasting and slicing. Still left is the setting of the table and the filling of the glasses. There is still so much left to do.

I stop. I look at myself, both the woman in the window and the girl in the backyard. I look at her, at us, and I realize something important. The girl who was moving through the rooms and among the aunts and uncles and cousins absorbing their voices, the girl who wasn't learning to cook, was learning something else.

That girl was learning to celebrate. That girl was learning to remember. That girl was learning to hold on and let go simultaneously. That girl was learning to be thankful.

DECEMBER 11, 2016

There are fewer and fewer leaves on the sycamore tree each day. More and more sky showing through the satin-smooth branches. Its neighbors in the backyard, two sawtooth oaks, are disrobing at a slightly slower rate, but they, too, are approaching nakedness. When the wind picks up, the trees sway and rattle, wiggle and rustle, like a little girl in a crinoline. An irritated liveliness. A frustrated animation.

Out of the corner of my eye I can see the shed, inside of which is an artificial Christmas tree that I intend, at some point, to drag into the house, stand in the corner, and decorate with baubles collected over the last forty years. Some of them are beginning to fade and fold. Some of them have a provenance I can no longer remember. Some of them I have kept only because they are big enough to fill the gaping holes in the plastic branches that, despite the manufacturer's assurances, are not the least bit lifelike.

I am struck suddenly by the incongruity. At just the time of year when trees, real trees, shed their leaves and step forth naked, we take pretend trees inside our homes, our stores, our churches, and we dress them. At just the moment when the sycamores and oaks and maples unconsciously demonstrate the loveliness of simplicity, we frantically rush to display ornamentation.

I look back at the tree, its remaining leaves waving frantically to get my attention. Forget what you think you know, it seems to be telling me. Forget the legend that says evergreen boughs on the hearth are reminders of the spring to come. Ask yourself why you attempt to contradict nature. Do you think that because your lamps repel the darkness and your thermostat rebuffs the cold, you are no longer at her mercy? Do you think you know so much that you can laugh at the cycle that demands a season of quiet, of dormancy, of death?

I do not like this line of questioning. I especially do not like the idea that a sycamore tree is the questioner, though I must admit that I am amused by the idea that it was, apparently, from his perch within such a tree that Zacchaeus was able to see what he could not have seen otherwise. Could it be the same with me?

It is Sunday. I have gotten up earlier than usual to get to church earlier than usual. Along with the young daughter of the associate pastor, I will perform the liturgy for the lighting of the Advent candle. This week it is the candle of peace. The unresolved conflict between naked trees and dressed trees has left me less than peaceful.

Now it is Monday and I pause before leaving for work to assess the sycamore's progress toward total defoliation. The empty branches are extended like scaffolding against the silver-gray sky, stretching like long arthritic fingers toward something I cannot see. There is a beauty in such bareness, a severe dignity in the act of uncovering the armature of a tree. Or a person.

And suddenly, with that thought I am Zacchaeus—seeing what I would have missed without the sycamore tree, understanding why we wrestle with the tree stand and tussle with the strings of tangled lights, knowing exactly where all the questions were meant to lead me, which is to the realization that it's not about the tree.

It's about us. We are the ones who are naked and we can no longer deny it. We are the ones who have lost our innocence. We are the ones who have been given the knowledge of good and evil and misused that knowledge to the detriment of our planet, ourselves, and our dreams.

We are naked and we are anything but unashamed. So we hide, not behind the animal skins of Adam and Eve but behind strings of twinkling lights and Christopher Radko ornaments, collectible nutcrackers and construction paper chains, sad representations of real stars and real angels. We fill the holes, gaping and otherwise, with shiny balls that are hollow and easily broken. We turn our bald spots to the wall and anchor ourselves with fishing line. And then we stand back and sigh unconvincingly, "So beautiful!"

Staring at my sycamore tree, I realize I don't want to do that anymore. I don't want to mask my empty places or prop myself up so that I look steadier than I am. I don't want to divert attention from my odd angles with spot lighting. I want to let go of the dead leaves so that, in the spring, there is room for new buds. I want to be a tree that lives in season, whatever the season may be.

DECEMBER 21, 2016

Up ahead, where the hard flatness of the highway drops off to a ragged edge, a large bird sits with his back to the white line. I am immediately cautious. Once, years ago when I was driving through Fort Stewart on my way to court, a huge black turkey buzzard, similarly situated just off the asphalt, abruptly rose into the air and then, equally abruptly, dove into my windshield.

The windshield did not shatter, but the rear-view mirror broke off completely. I sat on the apron of the road long enough to calm my shaking hands and to offer assurances to the nice man who had seen the whole thing and stopped to check on me that I was, in fact, okay. And then I drove on.

Since then, ever mindful of roadkill and its connoisseurs, I have been particularly alert to such things—things that move suddenly, that change course without warning, that defy expectation.

So no one can blame me when I take my foot off the accelerator, curl my fingers a little tighter around the steering wheel, glance quickly to make sure that the other lane is clear. No one can blame me for anticipating the worst and making preparation to avoid it. If the buzzard decides to forsake its noshing, I will be ready to slow, to swerve, to avert.

When I am about thirty yards away, the bird spreads its wings and begins to rise. At twenty yards away I can see it is not a turkey buzzard. At ten I recognize the deep brick color of the red-tailed hawk. I catch my breath as I watch him lift slowly above the wet grass, tail feathers flared and fluttering like a fan in the hand of a belle. Wings the breadth of a good-sized kitchen table fold and unfold, pushing the air down and away. In seconds he is gone.

I love red-tailed hawks. Love the way they ride thermals across warm spring afternoons and swoop effortlessly through pale autumn mornings. Love the way they embrace the solitude of sky dancing, twirling and spinning for their pleasure alone. Love the way they hold their heads so high and straight when they perch on power lines.

I don't know that I have ever been this close to one outside a zoo or wildlife refuge, and even though our encounter was of the briefest kind, I find myself smiling broadly as I accelerate. On a cold and rainy, gloomy and messy morning, I've just been handed a lovely gift. A lovely gift made lovelier because it contradicted my expectation.

Expectation is a big, important word at Christmas. Children expect Santa to grant their wishes. Mothers expect children to come home for a visit. Shoppers expect stores to be filled with bargains, and merchants expect shoppers to be filled with enthusiasm.

All of us, whether we willingly admit it or not, expect the lights and bows and tinsel and garland to somehow—Please, God, somehow!—make the hard things easier and the heavier things lighter. We expect the music and the cards and the Hallmark movies to ease the aches of our broken hearts and sand the edges of our difficult relationships.

That expectation, the one that exists despite all evidence to the contrary, the one that appears unbidden every single year right on cue, the one we can't avoid even when we know better, has a name. It is hope.

What did Emily Dickinson say? "Hope is the thing with feathers / That perches in the soul." Hope is the red-tailed hawk that isn't a turkey buzzard. It is a reminder on the side on the highway that what has always been true before does not have to be true this time. It is the tap on the shoulder that says, "Don't believe that the way it's always been is the way it always has to be."

I loosen my grip on the steering wheel and turn my gaze to the road ahead while, somewhere behind me, hope goes soaring through the December sky on brick-colored wings.

"I still preserve those relics of past sufferings and experience, like pillars of witness set up in travelling through the valve of life, to mark particular occurrences. The footsteps are obliterated now; the face of the country may be changed; but the pillar is still there, to remind me how all things were when it was reared."

—Anne Brontë, *Agnes Grey*

JANUARY 8, 2017

After the last decoration has been taken down, after the Fitz &
Floyd platters have been carefully shoved into the way-back of the
china cabinet, after the programs and pageants and parties have
been reduced to cleverly captioned images on Instagram, what is
left are the sounds. The real sounds.

Not the over-produced orchestrations of carols that sound-
tracked every moment of December, the ones with which the
crowds in the mall could only hum along because no one learns
the words anymore since school children get only thirty minutes a
week, if that, of music and when they perform it's a holiday con-
cert not a Christmas program. Not the ubiquitous jingling of
sleigh bells underscoring every commercial on every televised
sporting event, of which there were a multitude. Not the mind-
numbing beep beep beep of the barcode reader at Walmart, scan-
ning each of the individual items in each of the five overloaded
buggies that made up the shortest line available. No, not those
sounds.

The real sounds.

I was outside after dark, whispering with every step my gratitude for the balmy weather, smiling to myself over the good fortune of being able to walk around outside in January in shorts and
a t-shirt. It was cloudy. No moon, no stars. I walked at the edge
of the light, the edge of the darkness, the place where the artificial
glow coming from the house faded and my feet were just oblong
shadows.

I'd made a couple of loops around the perimeter when I
heard a cry, as plaintive a wailing as ever there has been. No banshee keening from the mounds of County Meath could have been
more bone-chilling. A single painful note unrolling over the field

like a fogbank. It stopped me in my tracks.

There was distance between us and I assumed it was some kind of bird, a night bird, a swamp dweller I had never heard before. I called myself brave and kept walking.

The cry got closer. I stopped again. This time it was obvious that the creature making the mournful sound was no bird. It sounded more than anything like a baby calf. But it couldn't be because, of course, we have no cows. I suspected it might be a fawn, a baby deer separated somehow from its mother. When I described it later to Keith, he agreed with my suspicion. "Sometimes," he said, "you can hear the mama answer back. Real soft like."

This wasn't one of those times. There was no cervine summoning of the child left outside playing past dark.

The cry eventually stopped, the baby—I assumed—having made its way to the doe's warm and heaving side to follow her across the field, making heart-shaped footprints all the way to the edge of the woods where they, as they do every night, would find a soft spot to nestle down and sleep. The rhythm of their days is steady, repetitive, not interrupted by holidays. They move from darkness to light, from one season to another in a cadence that makes every day holy.

I love Christmas. I love the gladness of gathering and the warmth of celebration. I love the rituals of the church and of my family. I love the way the oldest of things—ornaments and relationships and stories—are brought out into the open and caressed with the gentlest of hands.

But I also love the days after. The days when the rhythm of the ordinary returns. The days when the most beautiful trees are the ones lit not by twinkle lights but by the flame of a winter sunset. The days when the only carol breaking the silence is the song of an invisible fawn.

JANUARY 22, 2017

It has been a week of fog. The first morning, pushed slowly over the fields by a gentle breath, it made me think of the tendrils of smoke wafting from a cartoon Santa's pipe. The second it was flat, had the dull finish of an old car, and stretched from earth to sky in a single swath of mourning dove gray.

The third morning the kind lady on NPR warned of limited visibility and suggested caution on the roadways and, stepping out onto the front porch, I could see why. The previous days' fog had been almost intangible, practically two-dimensional, invisible except from afar. But this, this was thick and heavy and wet. It changed the shape of things and distorted distances. It fell on my arms and face and hair like a wave of depression.

It was so bad that, despite the instinctual alertness that comes from over forty years of dodging bucks and does and fawns, I did not see the dead deer lying smack dab in the middle of the dirt road until I was, quite literally, on top of it. Just as its soft tan coat, the exact color of the road, went under the front bumper, I simultaneously realized what it was, gasped out loud, and felt the car rise as though encountering a higher than usual speed bump.

The car was fine. I was fine. I have no idea about the vehicle that originally encountered the poor animal nor the driver thereof. I assume that he/she/it proceeded on through the vicious fog just as I did—slowly and respectfully.

It seemed at this point that I'd seen all the faces of fog. I was ready for a morning in which I did not debate myself all the way to work on the question of whether high beams or low beams were appropriate, in which Carl Sandburg and his little cat feet did not insert themselves into my thoughts every five minutes, in which—like the true flatlander I am—I could see the horizon and locate my place in the world. Still, I woke up again today to a landscape that couldn't be brought into focus simply by inserting my contact lenses. I could sense the imminent arrival of frustration.

Probably a direct result from frequent and intense contact with that particular emotion, what I've come to recognize as a feeling of annoyance at my own inability to change something that I think needs to be changed, I've learned that the most effective way of dealing with it is to be a good hostess. Open the door, ask it in, offer it a piece of pound cake and some sweet tea. Do that and frustration, like every guest who's ever been made safe and comfortable, will open up and tell you something you didn't know before.

So I walked out onto the porch and left the front door open, a sure sign of welcome. I took a deep breath and raised my arms, like you would if you were getting ready to offer your best friend a big hug. It was quiet and still, as though the fog had insulated the whole world. No birds chirping, no breeze tickling the wind chime. I brought my hands together under my chin, took another deep breath, and closed my eyes.

When I opened them, I could see the sun. Not a blazing orange smear, not a pink and lavender smudge, not a shimmering gold spread. What I saw was a white circle, a perfectly round sun, edges as sharp as a lens, smooth as a sphere. Like a biscuit-cutter biscuit. And I realized immediately that, but for the fog, but for the filter of all those billions and billions and billions of water droplets suspended in the sky, I wouldn't get to see that.

I love blazing orange smears. Pink and lavender smudges take my breath away. And shimmering gold spreads make me run for my camera. But there is more to acknowledge than the spectacular. There is more to notice than the flashy. There is more to see than what we can see.

I'm working hard to remember that. To remember it so well that I just know it. To remember it so well that I don't have to think about it. To remember it so well that the sight of fog will make me hungry for pound cake.

FEBRUARY 5, 2017

Like a blackboard on the first day of school, the night sky is flat and clean and dark. So very dark. The stars are strung from one horizon to the other in irregular clusters that, even to my own untrained eyes, look like pictures. Not archers and scales, but front-end loaders and salad tongs. Not lions and fish, but rakes and Christmas cacti.

About halfway up the sky to the west, the moon, a die-cut sliver of silver, hovers unusually close to two pulsing points of light that I have been told are Venus and Mars. The three of them light up that little section of sky like a neon sign. "Come hither," they beckon. "Join us. And if you can't join us, sit back and be amazed." And I am.

Back and forth from one edge of sky to the other, I turn my head and my eyes. I don't know that I have ever seen so many stars so clearly. The thought crosses my mind that this night, this sky, this lavish display of celestial bodies is quite possibly the most beautiful thing I have ever seen.

Which is why I am completely taken off guard by the next series of thoughts that come tumbling, stumbling, crashing, careening into my mind from somewhere. The thought that this breathtakingly beautiful sky is the same sky dangling over the 70-mile swath of towns and cities and fields and houses and highways less than 200 miles away that were left in ruins by a tornado bearing winds of somewhere between 136 and 165 miles per hour. The thought that this dazzling, bewitching, radiant sky is probably going completely unnoticed by the children who are sleeping on cots in a church fellowship hall and the mother whose two-year-old is still missing. The thought that the people who are wielding chain saws and axes and shovels during every daylight hour and falling asleep exhausted couldn't tell you and don't really care that Venus and Mars are so clearly visible.

And one more thought. A selfish thought. The thought that within that 70-mile swath there is a particular spot, a specific address, a place where I have been and belonged, a place that did not escape the destruction. And that thought dulls the brightness of the stars a little.

The people connected to that spot are long gone, relocated to other addresses, all happy and safe, but that does not preempt my sadness over knowing that the roof and walls that sheltered me have fallen. It does not prevent the editing of my memories. The feel of bare feet on tile floors is now accompanied by the imagined sight of those tiles broken and sticky with pine tar. The sight of a front door flung open in welcome is now paired with a ceiling caved in in submission. The sound of laughter and music is joined by the plaintive silence of a house left without people.

I realize in that moment that what I am feeling is loss—certainly—and grief, yes, but it is something more. It is empathy. And connection.

As I turn to go back inside, inside a house that is dry and secure and safe and mine, I feel a little guilty. A little shameful that I am so carefree as to be able to stand in my front yard and swoon over the night sky when so many people—the vast majority of the human beings on this planet—cannot. Because of poverty or displacement or illness or a hundred other burdens, millions of my brothers and sisters the world over do not have that luxury. And as long as they don't, I can never be complacent in the fact that I do.

It is one sky that shelters us all.

FEBRUARY 19, 2017

The fields surrounding Sandhill are naked. Along the edges of the yard, where a fence would be if I were a fence sort of person, the tractor tires have made loops like rainbows or rick-rack and I have to be careful not to stumble as I make my nightly rounds.

It is that time again. Time to start over.

It has been such a mild winter that I might have expected myself to be less moved by the sight of the fields stripped and plowed and cut and left waiting, less moved by this herald of spring. But I am not less moved. I may be, in fact, even more moved than usual.

In the wake of so few bitterly cold days, the turning under of naked cotton stalks seems less rebellious and more determined. Starting over, it reminds, does not always have to be in the wake of destruction or disappointment. Sometimes it is simply the natural order of things.

And, as I was reminded watching the television broadcast of the Grammy Awards, starting over can also be simply a matter of the desire to do one's best.

I don't watch awards shows much anymore. It may be because I have little time for the popular culture it celebrates, or it may be because the celebrations have too often turned into something completely other, platforms for the political opinions of those celebrated. Or maybe I just forget. Whatever the reason I generally don't watch, the reason I did watch this time is because I am a great admirer of Adele.

I explained my appreciation of the hugely popular singer to a friend of mine by saying that I especially like the fact that she just stands there and sings, that I can understand her lyrics without having to look them up, and that she makes me feel better about my body type. On Sunday night she added to that list of reasons for me to appreciate her artistry.

Chosen to perform a tribute to the late entertainer George Michael, Adele got off to a very rocky start. I am not enough of a musician to say exactly what was happening, but it was clear that discordant is the best way to describe it. So, on live television she stopped, apologized to the producer, used a swear word—for which she later apologized profusely—and said, "Can we please start it again? I can't mess this up." Later, accepting one of the three major awards she won that night, she said in explanation, "I had to get it right."

The Staples Center, where the ceremony was held, holds 21,000 people. Another 26 million people watched the broadcast. That is a lot of people in front of whom you admit you messed up, in front of whom you declare that this thing is important enough to start over.

Picking my way over the tractor tracks last night, kept company by yet another startlingly beautiful sky full of stars, I thought about starting over. I've done it plenty of times in the natural order of things—beginning new school years, celebrating holidays, planting gardens. And I've done it while experiencing excruciating pain in the wake of the deepest disappointment. But I couldn't remember the last time I had started over, from scratch, on something important, something public, something that mattered for no other reason than to get it right.

I decided I might need to do that occasionally. I might need to take a breath, look at what I'm doing—writing a column or planning a future—and give myself permission to start over for no other reason than my heart tells me that what I've done so far is out of tune. For no other reason than I want to do it right.

Adele started over and got a huge round of applause. One of those applauding was me.

MARCH 5, 2017

The first time I can remember standing in line was at the milk dispenser in the lunchroom at Mattie Lively Elementary School. I didn't like milk. I was not made to drink it at home. But in the lunchroom at Mattie Lively there was no other option.

So I stood there and waited my turn, took the metal cup holder from the rack, turned it upside down and pushed it hard on the stack of white paper cones. The cup holder was always cold, and it got colder as I lifted the handle on the milk dispenser and watched the stream of white liquid fall in.

Standing in line was a big part of what we did in first grade at Mattie Lively. We all got to be exceptionally good at it. I guess that's the whole point.

I left Mattie Lively fifty years ago and I'm still standing in lines. To place an order, to mail a letter, to buy a ticket. To make a purchase, to board an airplane, to receive a diploma. The line is often long and the movement slow. My companions are frequently people I don't know. But the result is that, generally, at the end of the line I've obtained or achieved something I desire. Rarely do I find myself in something like the Mattie Lively milk line, for a reason I don't like but for which there is no other option.

Rarely, but not never.

Saturday afternoon was beautiful. The sky was the blue of faded chambray and there was the slightest breeze. It didn't feel like February. I walked across the parking lot, hearing every step my dress shoes made on the gravel, bracing myself for what was ahead. I entered the building and took my place at the end of the line.

Over the next half hour or so I moved, along with my fellow line-dwellers, slowly, slowly, slowly forward, inching my way toward the moment when I would step in front of the husband and the three sons, each of them standing so ramrod straight that a stranger couldn't have guessed which one graduated from West Point. When my turn came, I would hug them and murmur something about how sorry I was for their loss, how much we all loved her, how much she loved them.

I hated being in that line. I hated the reason I was there. There was nothing good at the end of it, and yet there was no other option.

On Sunday morning, still hung over with sadness, I went to church. I sat through Sunday school and the sermon and then, without much conscious thought, there I was standing in yet another line. This time, though, I would be required to say nothing. This time, at the end of this line, all I had to do was receive.

"The body of Christ, broken for you." He broke off a piece of bread and dropped it into my outstretched hands. "The blood of Christ, shed for you." She held out the cup and I touched the surface of the dark liquid with the bread. It was a small morsel, but I could taste the salt in the bread and the bitter in the grape juice.

It is a little like tasting tears, this receiving of Communion.

And that is when I realized that there had, in fact, been much good at the end of the line the day before. In the sadness and the disbelief, the uncertainty and the fear, there was also communion—the bearing witness to an unfathomable loss, the attesting to memories that will forever defy that loss, and the affirming with every single tear that, in the end, it is what we share and how we share it that define what it means to be loved. What it means to be human. What it means to be alive.

MARCH 19, 2017

One bird feeder hangs from the still empty branch of a sycamore tree. One hangs from the already-budding branch of a sawtooth oak. Both feeders are full.

The birds that frequent these adjacent all-you-can-eat buffets have become braver in recent days. They no longer scatter like dandelion seeds when the back door opens. Instead they flit, without startle, to a perch close enough to their plates that they can watch my movements, know exactly when I've left the vicinity, and resume their meals.

We are not friends, the birds and I. We are neighbors. The kind who say hello at the mailbox, who are willing to pick up the newspaper when you're out of town, who remark on the new car in the driveway or compliment the new flowerbed, but who would never even think about being invited in for supper. Good neighbors.

One morning last week, just before the cold snap, I walked outside to see both bird feeders being patronized. A male cardinal, all slick and shiny red, stood proudly on the ledge of the feeder dangling from the sycamore tree. He gave me a quick glance and resumed his pecking, a man on a mission, not about to be deterred by something he'd long ago determined was not a danger.

A female cardinal, a color so close to the fresh new leaves of the oak tree that I did not see her at first, bounced quickly away from the feeder at which she'd been nibbling and landed on a nearby branch, her beak clamped onto a single sunflower seed. Her mate's bravado was matched by her caution.

Breeding season for cardinals starts in March, and since there was probably a nest somewhere nearby, the mother's glare was steady. Even as she raised and lowered her head in an effort to crack open the seed, I remained in the crosshairs of her tiny black eyes. Being the one responsible for filling the feeder did not, apparently, make me any less suspicious.

It was amusing to see such stereotypical gender roles being played out among the non-humans.

I kept thinking about my avian neighbors long after I left

them to their labors and drove off to my own, and my curiosity, or perhaps just my desire to be a good neighbor, sent me to Google and Wikipedia and all those intangible capitalized places—which have all but taken the place of the tangible lowercase places like library and dictionary and encyclopedia—to find out more. I found out that though the bird is most often called the northern cardinal, it is really a southern bird, and the first pair did not nest in New England until 1958.

I learned that cardinals are counted among the species of birds that "mate for life," but I also learned that the cardinal's average life span is one year. Comparing them to other birds known for lifetime monogamy—bald eagle, mute swan, whooping crane—and whose life spans average about twenty years, I found a difference significant enough to make me pull back a little in my admiration of redbird fidelity.

I discovered that cardinals do not migrate, that they are fairly social and join in flocks that may even include birds of other species, and that the brightness of the male's feathers is determined by the carotenoids in his diet.

What was most fascinating to me, though, especially considering my observation of protective mama cardinal and macho daddy cardinal, was the fact that both sexes of the cardinal, not just the male, sing. And their songs sound virtually the same.

In most other bird species, the male chooses an exposed perch, a stage, if you will, and offers up his version of a sentimental ballad, a stirring anthem, or a soothing hymn to claim his territory, while the female remains close by but silent. Not so the cardinals.

The cardinals' two voices multiply the melody and intensify the volume, announce in unison that they, the both of them, oversee their chosen province. Which means that my cardinals, the cardinals who had seemed so conventional, so traditional, so "Leave It to Beaver," were, in fact, the very model of modernity.

We are just neighbors, the birds and I. But in taking the time to get to know them, to eliminate the assumption that they are just like all the other birds, and to appreciate what makes them a little more like me, I can be a better neighbor.

And that is always one step closer to being friends.

APRIL 2, 2017

Across the way, two turkeys, dark and awkward, amble across the field. The larger leads, the smaller follows. Two mockingbirds dive-bomb the holly tree at the corner of the house as though the single berries on which they are intent are the last two berries on the face of the earth. Their wings flutter like the pages of an old book thumbed hurriedly. Somewhere in the near distance, a flock of geese squawk squawk squawk.

From the vantage of the back door it is hard to tell, but I think the two tiny birds teetering on the edge of the bird feeder and nibbling like polite ladies at an afternoon tea are Carolina wrens. Behind them, somewhere beyond the canopy of kudzu vines, small maples, and scraggly oaks that fall away to the pond, a duck calls out a single guttural note.

I am surrounded by birds this morning. I want to stand in the yard in the perfect spring air and still myself into a St. Francis pose in hopes that one or more of them will land on my shoulder, my head, my outstretched hand.

My friend Anne is a devoted birdwatcher, and I have to admit to a bit of envy when, over the years, she has recounted to our group of friends sightings of scarlet tanagers and goldfinches and indigo buntings, all colorful chaps that, as far as I can tell, have never been drawn to Sandhill.

A couple of years ago Annie became a Georgia Master Naturalist through the University of Georgia. They proclaimed her certified to share her knowledge of "the habitats, natural resources and the natural environments of our state" with the rest of us, making it even more evident to me that whatever I might think I know about woods and fields and critters, I am not, as Daddy would say, Ned in the first reader compared to her.

Which brings me back to the birds. As a consequence of her newly obtained knowledge and official recognition, I fully expected Annie to show off. In fact, I wanted her to do just that. I anticipated that the next time we were all sitting around on the wide porch of the big house on Signal Mountain where we do our best to flock once a year, we'd play something like a lightning round of Georgia Nature Bowl, during which of each of us would throw out a question and Annie would immediately bark back an answer.

"How long does a brown thrasher incubate her eggs?" "Anywhere from eleven to fourteen days. Next?" "How fast does kudzu grow?" "Up to one foot a day. Next?" "How many kinds of frogs are there in Georgia?" "There are thirty-three species of frogs and toads in Georgia. In addition, Georgia is home to more species of salamanders than any other place in the world, including the largest salamander in America."

It didn't exactly go like that. We were spread out across the porch in the rocking chairs, settled into the stillness of the mountain air, and looking out across the brow where the mist had just about obscured the view of Chattanooga, when somebody heard a bird somewhere off in the bushes.

Annie immediately identified the bird and then jumped up and hurried into the house, returning with her iPad. "Let's get him to come closer." In a few seconds she had swiped her way to a screen offering a picture of the bird she had identified. "Watch this," she said and touched the microphone icon.

The bird's song came streaming out of the iPad's speaker. In a moment the bird, the real bird, called out again, this time closer.

Three or four times the sequence was repeated, the iPad, like the Greek Sirens, calling again and again and the real bird answering, nearer and nearer. I don't remember who lost interest first, the bird or the women, but the call and response was the highlight of the afternoon.

Call and response. In music, it is two distinct phrases, one following the other and played by different musicians, in which the second is heard as a commentary on the main theme. In preaching, it is participation of the congregation, verbal encouragement, punctuation of the preacher's words. "That's right." "Amen." "Praise the Lord!"

Call and response. That is what the birds of Sandhill are initiating this morning. The mockingbirds and the geese and their brethren are calling. Calling me. They are playing the theme, preaching the sermon, inviting me to participate in the morning, this singular morning that regardless of its familiarity will never be again.

And my job, my one and only job, is to respond.

APRIL 16, 2017

There is one grapefruit left. One.

It sits in the wire basket on the counter along with five apples that are, quite frankly, past their prime. It is not quite yellow, not quite orange, and it is smudged with tiny dark lines that cross and knot like a web, that attest to the fact that it is not a grocery store grapefruit. It is not perfectly round or perfectly hued, but it is a grapefruit.

The others have already been scored and peeled, skinned and sectioned, bitten with lips drawn back in anticipation of tartness. This one, though, may be too dry to eat by now. I've passed by, looked at it over and over again, and yet I've chosen not to stop, not to get out the knife, not to take and eat.

I've just figured out why.

Cooper was a much-loved eight-year-old who liked to wear hats, especially fedoras. He shared a middle name with his aunt and a home with two sisters and a mother and father who described him as "an old soul." He endured far too many visits to doctors and hospitals with a huge smile and a sense of humor that most grown-ups would envy. In a world where smiles and humor are not that easy to find, his death made no sense.

Cooper's grandmother has been my friend for nearly thirty years. Thirty years and I realized, staring through the windshield into the haze on the interstate, that I had no idea what I would say to her when I walked into her hug.

From the parking lot of the Mulberry Street United Methodist Church where a group of us met to ride to the service together, we could see a passel of children on the playground, their voices rising and falling in some indeterminate key, all of them waiting for a mother or father to arrive, to grip a fat little hand in his or her own and lead the way home.

The poignancy of the moment, the unconscious tenderness of the parents with the children, underscored the reason why we had come, why Mary Catherine had driven from Signal Mountain and Anne from Blue Ridge and I from Sandhill, why Susan had raced down the interstate from Hartsfield, why others had forgotten whatever else they might have been doing on a Friday afternoon in March to make their way to Riverside Cemetery.

At some point, as we stood suspended in the surreality and the sunshine, Mary Catherine said, "I have grapefruit."

It turns out that her cousins who live in Florida had brought her grapefruit, lots of grapefruit, and she wanted to share. So each of us took a few. And I heard myself saying, "You know my motto: There is nothing in life so bad that it can't be made at least a little better by a party favor."

I immediately felt awful. It was a stupid thing to say. Totally inappropriate.

Except that now I know it wasn't. It was truth.

There are moments in life—moments of significant pain, deep uncertainty, or just the occasional awkward silence—when words are not adequate. When whatever power words might otherwise have to soothe anxiety, incite a political movement, or create the universe has been sapped. In those moments all we can do is share. Whatever we have.

I didn't say anything when I walked into my grandmother-friend's hug. I felt her head against my shoulder. I heard her catch her breath in a sob. I hugged her back. I cried, too.

Hugs. Tears. Grapefruit.

Here is a grapefruit. Here is my heart. Here are the memories we share and the grief that is now added to those memories.

Thank you. Thank you for the grapefruit. Thank you for this grace.

There is one grapefruit left. One. It needs no words.

APRIL 30, 2017

Poor Blanche Dubois. Always depending on the kindness of strangers. It is a dangerous thing, depending on the unknown. Much better—if one must depend at all, if one cannot be left to one's own devices—to depend on the kindness of friends.

This past week—in a five-day trek that took me to Macon, then to Kennesaw, then to Powder Springs, then to Lake Blackshear, and then back home—the kindness of friends accompanied me like a shadow.

It began with my visit to the English professor father of one of my oldest friends. It is a matter of both satisfaction and trepidation that he reads what I write and a matter of genuine pleasure to spend time with someone who, nearing ninety, still writes himself. Toward the end of our visit, he leaned forward and extended his hands toward me, palms open and facing each other, the gesture of someone intent on making his point. "I've been thinking," he said, "that you should get a dog. A big dog."

I felt a grin spread across my face. The writer had turned paternal on me. All my musings about wandering in the woods and rambling down dirt roads have made him worry for my safety. I assured him that I was careful, that my brother and my parents lived nearby, that I was, in fact, considering getting a dog. He sat back in his chair, content for the moment that I was in no danger, and when I left a few minutes later I did so feeling well tended.

Just a couple of miles down the road was Wesleyan and Alumnae Weekend where there would be no end of hugging and smiling and reminiscing. The friend in whose home I was staying had just experienced a significant loss and was in the midst of a major home renovation, and yet she managed, as always, to be the quintessential hostess. "You know where the Diet Coke is," she said. "Manage the thermostat to your liking," she said. "Make yourself at home," she said with every word and gesture. And I did.

On Sunday morning I drove to Kennesaw and had lunch with my niece Kate and her husband Kirck, a lunch that included an up-close look at the two of them teasing and laughing at each other with a sweetness I dared not mention to either, but which made my chest expand with happiness and which concluded with a purposeless and unhurried visit to a nearby Barnes & Noble. I left the store with four books to add to the stack at home and the giggly delight that there is someone, some two, in my family for whom wandering around a bookstore is as much fun as it is for me.

In Powder Springs I drove into a cul-de-sac, parked my car on the edge of the yard, and took out my umbrella. It is never easy to extend condolences and the wet gloom felt appropriate. Sandra and I have been friends for fifty years, and it was the death of her mother that had brought her from Indianapolis and me from Sandhill. Bad taste or not, we had one of Sandra's grown-up daughters take a photo of the two of us, and looking at that photo later all I could see was the little girls we used to be, the little girls who were so different from each other but who recognized the seeds of loyalty and faithfulness.

The final stop was Lake Blackshear, where the talk went late into the night, some of it significant and some of it frivolous, where I told the story of how my mother used to save the biscuits from supper and turn them into breakfast by slicing them in half, slathering butter on them, and toasting them under the broiler, only to wake up the next morning and find that my friend had done exactly that on the morning of my departure.

Back at home and sitting in a rocking chair on the front porch, I can take a deep breath and absorb the gifts of my trek around the state. The hospitality and the tenderness. The laughter and the tears. The questions and the answers. I can depend on those things. Those things and the fragile human beings through which they came, not one of whom is a stranger.

MAY 14, 2017

The holly trees have stood at either end of the porch for nearly fifteen years. They arrived in black plastic buckets, stubby and unimpressive, veritable runts compared to the proud sentinels they grew to be. I remember the delight with which I cut the first berry-bearing branches, so proud to be able to walk out the front door and gather from them my own Christmas decorations.

I have no idea when they grew so tall as to reach the corners of the house, so tall as to scrape the fascia boards when the wind comes roaring across the field rattling their branches. All I know is that they did, and one night I went out to replace what I thought was a blown floodlight only to discover that it was flooding light just fine, thank you very much. The problem was the obscuring of said light by the prickly green branches of a holly tree that had grown, silently and unobserved, into a nuisance.

When one lives in the country, far from streetlights and neon signs and strings of cars that send constant waves and arcs of halogen across the yard and through the windows, darkness becomes less an interference to regular activity and more a companion. Pushing the trash can to the road with no illumination beyond that of the stars becomes a reflection on the vastness of the universe. Walking to the mailbox under the light of a waning moon becomes a reminder of the tenderness of life.

But darkness can also be dangerous. One can, for example, turn an ankle in a hole dug by an armadillo while one is walking around after dark listening to the bullfrogs and trying to catch a whiff of lavender. So, after months of putting it off and only after being reminded by someone who was trying to be helpful that, as Charley Pride put it, snakes crawl at night, I had someone come out and trim back the holly trees so that I could actually see where I was going after sundown.

And by trim back I mean cut away everything green, saw off everything except the trunk and main branches, leaving something vaguely resembling the silver aluminum Christmas trees that used to adorn the store windows downtown in the 1960s. Not attractive at this point, but with the promise of resurrection and the assurance that I could wander around outside at midnight if I so desired with at least enough illumination to avoid serious bodily harm.

The next morning I walked out onto the porch, and the first thing I noticed was how quiet it was. The birds that generally greeted me with competitive singing had fallen silent. It took only a couple of seconds to realize why. And another couple of seconds to experience a wave of grief and guilt that nearly knocked me down.

It had never occurred to me that in eliminating—even if only temporarily—my own problem I was laying one at the doorstep of my neighbors. Not once did I think about the nests that might be, quite probably were, built in the branches that fell in heaps on the ground. Not once did I think about where the wrens and the swallows would rest, hide, sing.

And yet, even as an apology came rushing out of my mouth, I had another thought, an audible memory. I heard the voice of every flight attendant on every plane in which I've ever been a passenger: "Secure your mask on first, and then assist the other person." You can't, it is explained, be of help to anyone unless you have first assured your own safety.

The trees needed to be cut back. Not just for me, but for them as well. All living things need pruning and shaping eventually. But I still feel guilty.

I think the birds have forgiven me. They haven't stopped showing up at the feeders a couple of times a day and they haven't stopped singing. They just do it from perches in other parts of the yard. And I, with the assistance of unobstructed floodlights, am still walking around in the dark.

MAY 28, 2017

When Big Phyllis died, Lynn decided that, while flowers were nice and there was certain to be spray after spray from the Republican Women and the Daughters of the Confederacy and any number of other organizations to which Big Phyllis had offered her considerable talents and opinions, what the grave overlooking the bluff in Bonaventure Cemetery really needed was some water from Eagle Creek.

Eagle Creek isn't really a creek. It's a drainage ditch that runs along the edge of the football practice field at Georgia Southern University. A drainage ditch infested with gnats and such and imbued with magical powers by Coach Erk Russell who, during the playoffs in 1985, filled a milk jug with water from the ditch and sprinkled it in the end zone of the team's opponents. Georgia Southern won the national championship.

The sign erected at the edge of the ditch, just at the spot where players cross several times a day during practice, reads: "These mystical waters have traveled with teams of Eagles seeking championships and have become, in a short time, legendary. They reflect the unconquerable spirit of Georgia Southern, ever present no matter how far from home the Eagles soar."

Big Phyllis was a friend of Erk's and a huge Georgia Southern football fan, and I don't remember that I've ever said no to one of Lynn's ideas, so as soon as the funeral was over, she— Lynn, that is, not Big Phyllis (though if anyone could survive her own funeral that force of nature could)—and I headed to the drainage ditch that had been endowed with magical powers by nothing more than the words of another force of nature. My theory is that one of the reasons Erk and Big Phyllis were such good friends is that neither one of them ever gave much credence to the odds or put much faith in the pundits. They both knew that statistics can't factor in things like heart.

So there we were, in broad daylight, in front of God and four lanes of traffic on Fair Road, two grown women in what passes for funeral clothes these days, scrambling down the bank in our high heels, hers higher than mine. Right at the edge, thinking more of our shoes than our health, we slipped them off and tip-toed into the shallow brown water. I held one of Lynn's hands and leaned back toward dry ground as she leaned forward holding an empty plastic water bottle.

The graveside service was not until the next day and Lynn had to get back to Atlanta, so the actual delivery or, as we preferred to call it, the anointing of Big Phyllis's grave with Eagle Creek water was left in my solitary hands. As the gnats swarmed and the bagpipe player played, I held the bottle, whose contents looked a lot like a urine sample, unobtrusively down by my side.

At the final amen, I circled behind the casket, enlisting along the way the assistance of Big Phyllis's son-in-law to serve as shield; not everyone, we understood, would appreciate the appropriateness of the gesture. I opened the bottle, sprinkled some of its contents into the open grave, and emptied the rest on the ground around it. It has been a long time since I have felt such a sense of accomplishment.

Lynn's husband Lamar is not new to this circus and he, without complaint, documented the gathering of the water with a photograph. It is an image of two women smiling, two women looking straight into the sun, two women holding hands. I keep it on my phone.

The other night, as we were waiting for Chambless's preschool graduation program to begin, her big brother Jackson, who is practically a first grader now and for whom preschool seems ages and ages ago, took my phone and began scrolling through the photos. Most of them are of him and his sister—ball games and birthday parties, silly faces and serious gazes, holidays and regular days I was lucky enough to spend with them.

He stopped scrolling when he came to the photo of me and Lynn in Eagle Creek. He pointed and looked up at me. "Why are you standing in that water?"

I don't remember exactly what I told him—something about a football coach thinking it was magic—but the question has stayed with me, has continued to resurface in my thoughts over and over these last few days.

Why are you standing in that water? Why are you doing

something that no one else would understand? Why are you doing something that appears to have no purpose or no chance of success? And, for heaven's sake, why are you doing it so publicly?

The answer, I think, is the answer to all the great questions that start with why. Why was I standing in that water? Why am I standing in that water today and will I stand in it tomorrow? Because love compels me.

I, we, will never get beyond the boundaries of what we know and with which we are comfortable unless and until we are moved by love. And that is real magic.

JUNE 11, 2017

To make a tree, begin with a straight line, vertical. This is the trunk. On each side of the straight line add additional straight lines, shorter, at an angle. These are limbs. To the limbs add more straight lines, shorter still. These are branches. Continue in this manner until your tree is finished.

It is not difficult to master this skill. It is, in fact, a near-universal one. Long before a child learns how to put together a particular combination of lines and squiggles to make his or her name, that child knows how to draw a tree. Soft fingers curl around a crayon, a Sharpie, a pencil fat as an overripe stalk of asparagus. A head bends low over paper. Any child can draw a tree.

I don't ordinarily think a lot about trees when I am within sight of the ocean. Trees belong to the land, my anchor. The ocean belongs only to itself, my compass. But tonight is different. Tonight I find myself hovering between the two.

I am on the north end of Jekyll Island. The moon is an eyelash away from full, though it is a little hard to tell. A veil of gauzy clouds makes it look as though someone has taken an eraser to its edges. The dusk is heavy with dampness from the day's rain, threatening to make it the evening's. Along the dunes, the seagrass trembles in the slightest of breezes.

I am standing under a cluster of live oak trees. Stretching my neck to look up into the canopy they form over the wide green lawn, I notice that the trees—the ones whose very name distinguishes them from the ones I learned how to draw—every last one of them, have grown not straight and tall toward the sky but curved in the direction of the ocean.

This is not a characteristic of the species. There are thousands of live oaks all over the South growing upright and unbent, like yardsticks and arrows and two-by-fours. Planted somewhere else, the acorns that eventually became guardians of this island would have done the same. But they were planted here—by bird or man or God, who knows—and from the moment the first tiny twig cracked the soil, the wind created by the ocean has pushed and pushed and pushed against the will that would grow them straight.

It is still light enough for me to see the way the branches curl around and around, back and forth, stretching up and out toward the ocean like words written in Arabic. I am both anxious and curious in my ignorance of what they say.

I've been here before, on this exact spot. I can see and hear and smell and taste all that I saw and heard and smelled and tasted. I can feel what I felt. I stand very still and I am back in that other time. There is another full moon; children are laughing; I am wearing a black and white dress; the breeze is pulling at my hair pinned up off my neck.

I take a deep breath and return to the present as the translation of the trees' message moves through me like an electrical current: "For hundreds of years we have felt the wind. For hundreds of years we have borne its force. For hundreds of years we have yielded to its strength, but we have never given in. You won't either."

Across the way the waves slap at the shore and the needle of the compass quivers in delight.

JUNE 25, 2017

The first funeral home fan that I remember—probably from the funeral of a great-aunt or uncle, my attendance at which, as a child of four or five, would never in that time have been considered inappropriate—had a stock painting of Jesus as the Good Shepherd on the front. On the back would have been the name and address of the funeral home and a tasteful slogan along the lines of "Here when you need us" or "Treating your family like family for over 50 years."

In the decades since, I've wondered about things like whether there were dyes in the first century to make robes such a deep shade of blue and such a rich shade of red, but back then my wondering was limited to how long I was going to have to wear the crinoline.

These days funeral home fans don't always invoke the divine. Instead of Jesus standing at the door and knocking, some of my more recent acquisitions have featured bucolic scenes of a meadow, impossibly green, impossibly verdant, and necessarily generic. The unnamed locale could be an Appalachian valley, a New England orchard, or the Mississippi Delta in spring, just after a soaking rain.

Where it most definitely is not is where I am today—a sunscorched cemetery in south Georgia where wiregrass and cockleburs fight for space with the gravel rocks that tumble against each other under the tires of the hearse. Where I stand just outside the perimeter of the green tent under which the family is seated in metal folding chairs that still look exactly like metal folding chairs despite the fabric covers. Where I fan with the finesse of one bred to the task—elbow tucked against my ribs, wrist bent at a forty-five-degree angle and twisted slightly so that my palm is facing my chest, fingers curled loosely around the handle. Down and up, down and up. A regular beat. Like the one I've been taught is proper when administering CPR. The beat to "Stayin' Alive."

The fanning does little more than stir the hot air. My arms grow damp and a cling like Saran Wrap forms between my skin and my clothes. There is a kind gentleman standing next to me who pops open a black umbrella and moves a step closer. "This will help a little," he says, and it does. The shadow from the umbrella is dark and round.

The preacher reads a psalm, sings a hymn, shares a few remembrances of the departed. I can't make out every word from my vantage point where I'm trying hard not to step on someone else's grave. He says something, I think, about comfort for the grieving and that word—comfort—catches my attention.

A comfort. That is what the fan is. Not in a physical way, but in the way of being a solace in an uncertain world. It is a promise that, in a world in which so much has changed, is changing, will continue to change, some things haven't, don't, and won't. "Here," says the kind face in a dark suit. "Take this thin yet sturdy piece of cardboard with a balsa wood handle and be reminded that some things last. It won't keep you cool, but it will keep you sure."

The preacher says amen and I walk toward the car where a quick blast from the air conditioner vaporizes the sweat and replaces it with chill bumps. I slip the funeral home fan up over the visor where over the next few days it will slide back and forth until, eventually, it will fall gently to the seat beside me.

I will reach over and pick it up, think back to the funeral, the heat, the gentleman with the umbrella. And I will feel it again, the comfort. I will turn off the air conditioner and fan, fan, fan.

JULY 9, 2017

Second grade was the year I asked for and got a stuffed French poodle for Christmas. I named her Fifi. She had thick wire in her legs and could stand on my dresser by herself. It was the year that Mama made me a pink pin-wale corduroy dress for the Valentine's Day party at school. It had a Peter Pan collar and a high yoke with tiny pearl buttons down the front. It was the year that I added to my vocabulary the words college, scholarship, and author and decided that those words were mine.

It was in first grade that I took my first tentative steps out into the world, but second grade was the moment when I realized my autonomy, my separateness, my ability to experience things and feelings distinct and apart from my family.

One November afternoon, sunny but with the dullness of fall, the brown wooden box on the wall at the upper left-hand corner of the chalkboard crackled to life. "Attention please," said Mr. Adams, our principal. "Teachers, attention please. President Kennedy has been shot." And he placed the big silver microphone near a radio from which a scratchy voice offered up the first reports of what had just happened in Dallas.

I remember Peggy Franklin crying. I remember Mama holding the screen door open as I stepped off the bus, her face drawn and tears sliding down her cheeks. I remember sitting in a big leather chair at my grandfather's furniture store on West Main Street watching the flickering gray television images of horses and soldiers moving slowly down the street in what I recognized as Washington, D.C. I remember John John in his little double-breasted coat saluting his father's casket.

I remember the rapid expansion of my vocabulary to include assassination, motorcade, and cortege.

A couple of weeks ago I happened to be in Dallas for a few hours with a friend and her two grown daughters. Our hotel was just a few blocks away from the site of the assassination and we decided to pay a visit. The concierge at the hotel handed us a map and pointed out the spot. Dealey Plaza.

In five minutes the four of us were standing on the sidewalk where, over fifty years ago, crowds had stood and waved and cheered the handsome young president and his beautiful wife in her pink Chanel suit. We could see the building that used to be the Texas School Book Depository. We stood on the grassy knoll.

Sandra and I shared with her girls what we remembered. One of them remarked that they'd not covered the Kennedy assassination in school. Probably, I told her, for the same reason that we never got to the Korean War. We ran out of time.

I've thought of that conversation a lot since I got home, thought of it in connection with the admonition that Moses offered the children of Israel as they set out to take the Promised Land. It's important to remember, he told them. It's important to tell your children what happened before. Rehearse it in their ears. Over and over. Tell them the stories. The good ones and the bad ones. The victories and the defeats. The moments when the human spirit triumphed over despair and the moments when despair seemed—for the moment, but only for the moment—to win.

We must tell them. We can't leave it to their friends or the schools or the churches. We can't leave it to the news media or social media or any other media. It is up to us, the adults who love them. And we have to end those stories not with a happily ever after but with the truth that we can't always predict what's next, but we can always know that hope never runs out of time.

JULY 23, 2017

The first day it rained. The second day it rained. The third day the sun came out, slowly and sheepishly, as though embarrassed by her failure to perform earlier in the week. The beach swelled with people, families mostly, and toys of various sizes and costs without which the vacationers would have had to notice the ocean or, worse, engage in conversation.

My friends and I planted our chairs a few feet above the water line, cognizant of the rising tide and the probable necessity of moving them up the sand at some point in the not distant future. The waves rushed and fell back, shouted and then lapsed into a whisper. Over and over. Back and forth. I could feel myself slowing, like a yo-yo hurled from a curled fist and left to unwind, its movements growing shorter and less violent with each up and down. Breaths growing deeper, muscles relaxing, thoughts quieting.

It lasted about ten minutes.

"I need to walk," I told my friends as I laced up my tennis shoes. I headed south.

It was late afternoon and I'd spent most of the week listening to lectures on topics like "Cyberbullying" and "Trying the High-Profile Murder Case." I'd seen images and heard words that I wanted to bleach from my memory. I'd been reminded over and over that evil exists and that the defense against its advancing tide is only as strong as the hearts of the men and women holding the line. I think I can be forgiven for feeling less than joyous.

I passed two elaborate sand fortresses under construction, a sailboat faded by salt and sun, a stick-drawn beach volleyball court, and tent after tent shading people of every size and shape and color, immobile and, for the most part, silent. It was as though, exhausted by the process of getting themselves and their children and the coolers and towels and tents to the beach, they had collapsed just a few yards short of the object of their desires.

Farther down the beach, in front of the grand old hotel, the row of blue canvas chairs shielded by blue canvas umbrellas, military in the precision of its line, held more still and silent people.

Their faces were hidden by sunglasses as they stared straight ahead, not moving, barely breathing. Even they, with the ease of wealth and the service of other people, exuded the air of, if not despair, at least lethargy. As though nothing, not even this brilliant summer day at the edge of the ocean, was enough.

I had just turned around to head back to my friends when a little boy, no older than three or four, darted from the shadows of one of the tents directly in front of me. I had to stop to avoid hitting him. He was at top speed and never saw me. There was a huge smile on his face and I watched him run as hard as he could toward the water, oblivious to anything else. He knew what he wanted, he knew where he was going, and he was delighted by it all.

Within the span of those few seconds, I felt my spirits lift, my attitude adjust, my outlook improve. I am decades past three and I've lived far too long to be oblivious, but the little boy's compact embodiment of joy reminded me that there is absolutely nothing to prevent me from knowing what I want, knowing where I'm going, and being delighted by it all. I can be the little boy, arms flailing and legs pumping, sprinting toward the wild and endless ocean.

All it requires is choices and intuition. Both mine.

I may fail. I may not reach my goal or get what I want. There will still be evil and darkness and injustice in the world, but from my place in the line the world will see a reflection of the sun.

AUGUST 6, 2017

Mama didn't buy Jell-O. Not even to adorn with a can of fruit cocktail and call it salad. The only time my brother Keith and I got Jell-O was at school, cut into a square and plopped into a perfectly sized compartment on one of those indestructible oblong trays.

I was probably eleven or twelve when I saw the first commercial about Jell-O 1-2-3. I was absolutely mesmerized by the assertion that one could mix the contents of the handy packet with water, put it in the refrigerator in a tall glass—preferably, it would appear, one with a long stem—and come back later to a lovely and delicious parfait, a three-layered delicacy that included "creamy topping, fluffy chiffon, and cool, clear gelatin." I somehow convinced my frugal mother to buy this amazing product and proceeded to create what I was sure would be a food so sophisticated that it would somehow enable me to overcome all the impediments—too tall, too smart, too religious—that stood between me and popularity.

The result was not as amazing as the marketing. The top layer, which I expected to be a lighter version of the meringue Mama whipped up from egg whites for Sunday's lemon pie, tasted like much of nothing. It collapsed in my mouth, leaving behind the faintest hint of artificial strawberry flavor.

The second layer, the "fluffy chiffon" for which I had such high hopes, was okay. It reminded me a lot of pudding except without the richness of pudding or the thick feel of milk and eggs heated and stirred so slowly that the result was neither solid nor liquid, but simply a heavy presence of deliciousness dissolving in your mouth.

And the bottom layer, well, it was just Jell-O.

This is what I am thinking of when I walk out onto the porch in the early morning, look across the field, and see the first indication that summer is packing its bags in anticipation of its departure. The sky is layered. Like a Jell-O 1-2-3.

The clouds are white like cotton batting, like cotton candy, like cotton balls glued to construction paper to look like clouds. They start at the top of the pine trees at the property line, stretching straight up to wherever the top of the sky might be. Underneath the clouds is a layer of fog, dull silver like a tray in need of polishing. It hovers between the treetops and head-height of a good-sized man. And under that is the mist, the damp translucent mist that makes the domed rows of peanut vines glisten in the morning light.

It is hard not to laugh at myself, laugh out loud. Where do these thoughts come from?

It is 7:30 in the morning. I am standing on the porch catching my breath before leaving for work. I am looking at a peanut field shrouded by clouds. An image from nearly fifty years ago jumps to the front of my mind, an image I did not know existed. What does it mean?

I don't know. Yet.

There is no offering of regrets to memory's RSVP. It will, without permission or the necessity of a token, transport you faster than any time machine to a moment, a breath, a blink that changed everything. Or didn't. It can tickle or scald, bless or scold. It is simultaneously seductive and frightening, luring and repelling, even as you realize that it can be none of those things without your acquiescence. It is, after all, yours.

The Jell-O parfait, sophisticated though it may have been, did not make me popular. Nor particularly sated. What it did do was give me a template to lay over a morning sky some fifty years later, a way to see differently something I see every day, and a realization that what the quantum physicists say is true: past, present, and future are all right here, right now. We haven't lost a thing.

AUGUST 20, 2017

I am four or five years old. My arms are curled tightly around my father's neck. His arms are wrapped around my waist. We are standing in the Ogeechee River, wide and dark, brown as coffee. The trees that grow along its banks are tall and heavy with branches that dangle over the river, dripping Spanish moss. On the sandbar just a few yards away, my family—aunts and uncles and cousins, grandparents, my mother, my brother—move around in a cone of sunshine, a spotlight cutting through the canopy of cypress and pine and scrub oak.

They are laughing and talking. The children are running back and forth, splashing at the edge of the water. It is bright and noisy where they are. But where we are—my father and I—it is dim and quiet. It is peaceful. It is a different place. This is my first, my oldest memory of not just being outside but of being IN the world.

I have conjured this memory—and I do mean conjured as in pulling it up with a kind of spell, an incantation of wondering and a potion of solitude and quietness—as I work on remarks I am scheduled to give to an environmental group. My topic is "How to Make an Environmentalist."

I have no idea why I suggested that topic. Do I even know what an environmentalist is?

A word loaded with meaning, it is used by people of widely varying stripes with alternately positive and negative connotations. It is a word like "artist," "Southerner," "liberal," "athlete," or "Christian," heavy with history, both personal and societal.

Is the "artist" a photographer or a classical pianist? Is the "Southerner" a descendant of the First Families of Virginia or a wiregrass farmer? Is the "athlete" a member of the PGA tour or someone who goes to the gym every day after work?

I decide that an environmentalist is a person who has a significant emotional or historical attachment to a particular place, an attachment that motivates him or her to work to preserve that place. I also decide that I am one.

An environmentalist, at least this one, takes a while to make, but in that first, oldest memory I can see the recipe and the ingredients. First, I notice how young I was. Four or five. My attention had not yet been captured by the socialization of school. My entire world was my family. Where they went, I went. What they liked, I liked. What they honored, protected, and appreciated, I would learn to honor, protect, and appreciate.

Second, I notice how I felt. Held securely in the arms of someone I trusted implicitly, without even knowing what trust was, I knew no fear. And knowing no fear, I could absorb the sensory elements of that experience, absorb and retain them for the rest of my life.

Third, I notice where I was. The Ogeechee River is right down the road. It is the spot to which the people I know are referring when they say "the river." No one needs to ask which one. It is just a river, but it is ours and therein lies its great value.

Early exposure through a trusted adult in a comfortable and familiar place. The rain and sunshine and fertilizer that turned my innate connection to the earth, a connection every human has, into a great love. That made me an environmentalist.

This is what I will tell them, the people who have asked me to share my thoughts. This is what I will tell them and suggest that they go provide the rain and sunshine and fertilizer for a child they know. This is what I will tell them with the prayer that we all become, all remain environmentalists.

SEPTEMBER 3, 2017

The rain lasted long enough to move the sky from dusk to hard dark, to leave the grass glistening, to flatten the anthills out by the mailbox. Long enough for me to notice when the sound reduced itself to the monotonic drip drip drip from the eaves and the cones streaming from the floodlights on the corners of the house went from pale and thick to bright and golden. Just long enough to make the night an invitation.

I accepted.

The toad on the front steps hurried away into the shadows as my footsteps approached. Straight toward the road I headed, making a sharp right at just the point where the grass meets the dirt. I followed the edges of the yard, around and around and around—along the field road to the branch, down the row of trees to the shed, then back toward the road along rows of peanuts slurping in the just-fallen rain.

My steps grew more confident as my eyes adjusted, better able to avoid the ridges left by tractor tires, the holes left by armadillos. I could make out the faintest glow of the moon, shrouded by deep shadows. As I got closer to the back corner of the house I could suddenly smell the strong, piquant scent of rosemary resurrected from a severe pruning and the equally strong but sweeter scent of Russian sage. I came up short and stopped, took a deep breath, and wondered if the rain had somehow released the scents, if the still-heavy humidity was concentrating them into this small spot.

I walked until the wet seeped through my tennis shoes, through my socks, until I could feel my toes beginning to shrivel. I didn't want to go inside. I wanted to keep walking in the dark.

At my desk, taking one last look at the incessant stream of information that technology affords, I noticed an Instagram post from Brene' Brown, a researcher and author whose work on shame and resilience, being vulnerable and showing up has had a significant impact on the way I look at the world and myself. Brene'—because I think of her as a friend—lives in Houston and is right in the middle of the loss and displacement and fear and uncertainty gifted to southeast Texas by Hurricane Harvey, and her post, a video made at the NRG Center, showed us a woman who wasn't trying to hide any of it. Her hair was spiky and she was wearing no makeup.

This is what she said: "Everyone has been asking what you can do to help. I'm going to ask you for what we really need because this is not a community that needs anything to be pretty or wrapped in a bow. We need underwear."

Then she gave people the link to Amazon where they, where I could buy underwear—clean, fresh-smelling, never worn underwear for the people of Houston. So I clicked and clicked and clicked. And I filled my Amazon cart with underwear and I clicked one more time to send them on their way.

And then I went to my Facebook page and I wrote a post about praying for Houston, but not being satisfied with just praying. And I wrote about Brene' Brown and being the person in the arena and I shared the link and I asked my friends to buy underwear.

And they did. Within minutes, the responses to my post started showing up. People buying underwear for people they do not know, will never meet. People whose age, race, and religion are irrelevant. I couldn't help crying.

In the strangest form of alchemy I'd ever seen, I watched as the compassion of my friends, my family, my people transformed into action, their prayers turned into underwear. In the midst of flood and deepest darkness, mercy manifested itself like the scent of rosemary and Russian sage rising through the night.

SEPTEMBER 17, 2017

When the click and flicker that signaled the loss of power sent the house into dimness and silence, I thought about going through the rooms and turning everything off. Then I realized I wasn't sure exactly what had been on, which lamps, which ceiling fans, which ceiling lights. All that light—all that automatic, instantly available, taken for granted light—and in less than ten seconds I'd forgotten which of the many switches produced it.

The power came back on some twenty-five hours later, just after noon. I went through the house and, turning them off as I went, counted the lamps and overhead lights that were suddenly blazing again. One, two, three…eleven, twelve. Had it really been that gloomy and gray as Irma's wide arms flailed wildly outside my windows? So gloomy and gray as to require that much light to beat back the darkness?

I didn't spend much time on the contemplation. The sun was forcing its way through the clouds, so as soon as I could get the towels that caught the leak from the ceiling up off the floor, I was outside to greet her. It didn't matter that the rocking chairs were clogging up the guest room and the deck furniture was jammed in the shed and all those towels needed washing. All that could wait.

The first thing I noticed was that the air was thick with the smell of peanuts, a mixture of nitrogen and dirt, that strange perfume that signals the beginning of fall. I heard, in the distance, the call of geese. And, there, high in the sky, exactly where she is supposed to be was the sun.

Light. Bigger than Hurricane Irma. Brighter than LED.

Sandhill is nearly twenty-six years old. Studying the blueprints with the builder I pointed at every window. "Bigger." "Longer." "More." He accommodated me.

For at least fifteen years they were completely unadorned. No curtains. No blinds. I wanted to be able to sit anywhere, stand in any spot and see the slant of light falling in straight lines across the floor, in even curves across the back of the couch. I monitored the seasons by the angle at which the moonlight came through the window of my bedroom.

I didn't care that it faded fabrics and wood. I didn't care that it increased my power bill. And, honestly, I didn't care that people thought it was odd.

Grannie came to Sandhill one day and noted, "Darling, you don't have anything up to your windows."

"I know, Grannie. I like it that way."

"But what if somebody was looking in?" Her tone of voice held both genuine curiosity and abject fear.

"Well, Grannie," I offered in a moment of cheekiness never to be repeated, "if they come this far, they deserve to see something."

I don't think she ever got over it. But I hope she understood that my need for light is greater than any apprehension I might have of being observed.

Though I'd never thought of it in metaphorical terms before the visitation of Hurricane Irma and the waiting for EMC and the remembrance of that visit from Grannie, I've decided that one of the truly grand things about growing up and growing older is learning that how one may appear to others is never worth apprehension.

It is no reason to hide behind curtains, no reason to wear a mask, no reason to pretend to be anyone other than who you are. No reason to stand anywhere but in the light.

OCTOBER 1, 2017

It was a gift from Daddy's friend Frank Simmons when we first moved out to Adabelle in 1974. It was supposed to be— "supposed to be" taking on the colloquial Southern meaning of "presented with the understanding and belief that it was"—a silver-leaf maple.

It didn't take long for everybody concerned to figure out that it wasn't, like a lot of things, what it was made out to be. It didn't take long because a sycamore tree, which is what it was, will grow like a weed under the right conditions, and apparently Mama and

Daddy's backyard offered excellent conditions.

Over the years we decided that it was all just as well. That sycamore became an excellent climbing tree for Adam and Kate, and the flower bed Mama made around its trunk burst forth in the spring with a wild mess of daffodils and red amaryllis that could have made a beautiful cover for *Southern Living*. We were never much for raking leaves at our house, so when the leaves, big as a grown man's hand, starting falling and floating through the autumn sky, we ignored the mess and just enjoyed the rustle and crunch as we walked through them.

I was always particularly enamored with the bark, the way it peeled off in long sheets and left the tree smooth and cool. It made me think of the Native American canoes in my elementary school social studies books, and I imagined how it could have been used like papyrus to send messages or record stories. I didn't know then that the peeling accompanied growth.

Years later, after I'd built my own house, I came home one afternoon to find Mama and Daddy in my backyard, huddled around a fingerling of a tree with a couple of bright green leaves sprouted at the top. "We brought you a sycamore," Daddy pronounced as he stomped around the freshly turned dirt with his work boot. "This all right?" he asked, pointing at the tree and referring to the location. It was, of course.

That tree is somewhere around fifteen years old now. Maybe a little older. I don't know for sure. What I do know for sure is that it is old enough to have become an elegant and more than adequate shade tree for Sandhill and young enough to still look small compared to Mama and Daddy's.

I walk under its branches every afternoon as I make my way around the yard, and at a certain point, looking from a certain angle, and when the field in between is growing peanuts not corn, I can see the other sycamore tree at the same time. The older house with the bigger tree and the newer house with the smaller tree. It reminds me of the elementary school primers with which we learned to read the words big and little, tall and short, old and new.

Opposites, our teachers told us. These things are opposites.

But our teachers were wrong. I am standing under my syca-more, and one of its limbs has gotten tangled in my hair. I reach up to pull it loose, to brush away the fading leaves that fall across my cheek, and I realize that, in the context of living things, there are no opposites. Only movement. Little turns into big, short grows into tall, new will eventually be old.

Whatever it appears to be today, it may well be something else tomorrow. Or next year. The joy may turn into pain, the loss into gain. The silver-leaf maple may become a sycamore. It is in-cumbent upon us only to watch and listen, to pay close attention to the metamorphosis that is happening in every moment. Watch and listen and write it all down on the peeling bark.

OCTOBER 15, 2017

Scene 1: A snail shell sits still and alone on the concrete of the car-port at Sandhill. It is about an inch and a half long, the color of coffee diluted with lots of milk, with the slightest sheen. I don't remember the last time I've seen one. I am entranced.

I pick it up to ascertain whether it is occupied. If it isn't, I will take it inside and set it somewhere—the windowsill in the kitchen, most likely, but maybe the bathroom counter or on a lit-tle dish on my desk. If it is occupied, I will simply put it down.

It is occupied.

Four days later I return from a weekend in the mountains. I see the shell again. It is about eight inches away from where it was before. It brings new meaning to "snail's pace." I have a lot of things to unload—a too-full suitcase, a bird's nest fern, a tote bag, a pocketbook, trash. I want to be careful not to step on the snail, so I move it out of the path from car to back door.

I make one trip. Two trips. Back and forth. I get distracted. I hear the sharp crack and jump. For a moment I cannot make myself look down. The fragile shell has shattered beneath the weight of my shoe, the weight of me. The gelatinous clump that was the snail makes a small stain on the concrete as I cry out, "I'm sorry! I'm sorry! I can't believe I did that! I'm sorry!"

Scene 2: There is nothing more beautiful than a peanut field at full maturity. Rows of emerald green stretching to the horizon, unrolling like rick-rack in smooth, even curves. The beauty is short-lived though. The tractor idles in the field road, diesel engine coughing. It eases into the first row and lowers the peanut plow, long thin fingers of metal that will gouge the earth, reach deep into the roots of the peanut plants and hoist them from the cool dampness into hot dry October.

The green disappears, hidden beneath the browns and grays of peanuts and dirt. The curves flatten. The sun absorbs the moisture, turns the vines dry and brittle. They shrink and fall into flat piles. They die.

Scene 3: It is any day on the farm. I will find a feather or an acorn or a leaf. I will pick it up and look closely at its barbs, its cap, its veins. I will run my fingers over its surface. Each one—the feather, the acorn, the leaf—will have fallen from where it started. It will have lost its grip.

In a few weeks I will celebrate Sandhill's twenty-sixth anniversary. Twenty-six years since the last nail, last shingle, last wire magically melded to create a house. Twenty-six years of sitting on the porch watching deer graze on peanuts, standing at the kitchen window watching sunsets, sitting at my desk watching the moonrise.

And twenty-six years of watching corn twist in drought, roads wash out in flood, trees explode in lightning strikes.

What one learns from such observation—extended and intense—is that beauty is found not just in the beautiful. It is found in devastation and destruction, in darkness and death. In dull middles and painful endings. In losing what you cannot live without. In living with what you cannot change.

In settling gently to the ground like a feather. An acorn. A fallen leaf.

OCTOBER 29, 2017

The late afternoon sun made my shadow long and narrow. It stretched out in front of me like a plumb line. I had brought with me no book, no iPod, nothing to mute the sound of my shoes crunching like cereal on the dirt that just the day before had been mud.

A few yards ahead, startled by my approach, a covey of quail flushed from its hiding place in the broom sedge. The flutter of twenty wings sounded like pages of a book—thick and well-worn—falling from beneath a thumb's stroke. They rose and scattered, some of them barely clearing the vegetation. One of them flew head-height across the road in front of me, its soft brown body a smudge against the sky.

They are such vulnerable creatures. Shy and elusive, they generally depend on their camouflage to protect them, crouching and freezing when threatened, and they fly only when danger is close. And yet they like to live on the edges of things. Edges of fields, edges of forests.

Edges are perilous places.

There is a photo on the windowsill of my office. A sunset over Goulds Inlet, one of my favorite spots on my favorite island. My boss took the photo and gave it to me, aware of my affinity for sunsets and Saint Simons.

This morning he came to the door to ask a question, make a comment, alert me to something, I don't remember what exactly. "Nice photo," he quipped, pointing to the one on the windowsill. And from there our conversation slipped and slid from one place to another until we were talking about erosion and accretion, the falling away and the building back.

"Edges are fragile places," I said.

I visited some friends this weekend, friends who enfold me, warm me, feed me. Friends who care not one whit what irritations I bring with me, what impatience I pack in my suitcase, what impertinence and frustration and general human-being-ness I drag through the front door. They care only that I am there and I care only that they have welcomed me.

We have loved and laughed and lived not just from the sweet center of existence, the place where the heart beats strong and steady and the sun shines long and hard and the future cannot possibly be anything but wondrous, but also from the edges. The perilous edges. The fragile edges.

Places where hearts and bodies and wills were pushed to their limits. Places where camouflage was not enough to forestall danger, where erosion ate away at foundations. Places where the dirt crunching beneath our feet was broken dreams.

And this is what I have learned: I would rather live on the edges—the perilous, fragile edges. Because it is how we live, what we do on the edges, that determines whether we are men and women of courage or cowardice, faith or fear. It is how we face the attacks—with shattered shields or no shields at all—that measures the depths of our dreams. And it is with whom we face them—those who know the edges rather than those who huddle in the center—that makes the battle, regardless of its outcome, worthwhile.

NOVEMBER 12, 2017

The sun has not yet cracked the tree line. Its blush is just beginning to show when I step out onto the front porch to gauge the day. The air is close and the bird song is clear. Whatever I hear, see, feel today, I will hear, see, feel sharply. This much I know.

I must leave home early this morning for court in Jenkins County. I will cross the Ogeechee River to get there and it occurs to me, as it has countless times over these many years, that whenever I leave Bulloch County to go to Effingham or Jenkins or Screven, whenever I "ride the circuit," as we used to say, I always have to cross the river.

That thought is especially poignant today, All Saints' Day. The day on which the Christian church remembers all those who have died in the faith. The day on which "Shall We Gather at the River" is the hymn of choice and no one seems to notice that using a river as the metaphor for the afterlife sounds more than vaguely like Styx in Greek mythology.

In this thoughtful and near-melancholy state—a mile and a half from home but still on the dirt road—I am jolted by a flicker of movement off to the right. I slow an already slow car to allow the deer I cannot see yet to cross my path. He bounds from the field edge, over the ditch, hitting the road once with his hard hooves and bounding into the woods on the other side. Before I can accelerate, a squirrel who could have easily been crushed by one of those hooves darts across the road in the opposite direction.

I pause for a moment, my foot on the brake, to consider what I've just observed. One large animal, one small, spurred to movement simultaneously. Both panicked into moving directly into the path of danger. Neither would have been at any risk from me or the thirty-five hundred pounds of metal and plastic I was navigating had he simply remained where he was—deer in the open field, squirrel in the underbrush. Neither would have found his heart thumping wildly, his extremities quivering had he kept still and allowed the traffic, albeit a single car, to simply flow on by.

I wonder how many times I have been the deer, the squirrel. How many times I've heard an unfamiliar noise and responded to it with fear just because it was unfamiliar, not because I had any reason to believe I was in peril.

I drive on. I cross the river. I go to court. I cross the river again on my way back. I don't notice it when I cross, not even the sign stuck in the ground at the edge of the pavement.

My thoughts are preoccupied with the deer and the squirrel and the paradox on which I've stumbled as I consider that they ran from opposite directions. The side of the road from which the deer escaped was the side to which the squirrel ran for cover. The side from which the squirrel was flushed in fear was the side on which the deer found camouflage. Can both sides be simultaneously safe and dangerous?

I drive on and the paradox morphs into the tender idea that leaving doesn't always have to be about avoiding danger and arriving doesn't always have to be about seeking safety. Sometimes it's not even about leaving and arriving. Sometimes it's simply about the crossing itself. About the spot exactly halfway across the bridge where the view is better than anywhere else. About the moment when all four of the deer's hooves are in the air and he is, without a feather to his name, flying.

So, yes, we will gather at the river. And with any luck, we will cross it by leaping straight into the sky.

NOVEMBER 26, 2017

Confession: I set the table primarily for myself. The good dishes and the brass candlesticks and the tall tapers. The cloth napkins rolled and threaded into napkin holders. The broom sedge or cotton stalks or whatever I've foraged from the fields around the house staked into vases and pitchers and crocks.

I do it because I like the way the sunlight reflects off the creamy white china and the way the candle wax puddles and quivers for a split second before plunging over the edge in a long, slow stream. I do it because I like the heft of the glasses, the forks, the knives in my hands as I circle the chairs to drop them into place. I like the way the wrinkles on the tablecloth stretch and smooth underneath the weight of all the plates and platters.

This predilection does not reflect the Thanksgiving tables of my childhood. Grannie's table, cleared of the white crocheted doily and bud vase of plastic flowers and covered with the roasting pans and Corningware dishes and thick crockery bowls that held the day's feast. The tables at which the men gathered first to eat quickly and ravenously of the turkey and dressing, creamed corn, sweet potato souffle, and chicken and dumplings. The tables around which, after the men had gone outside to play pitch penny in the autumn sunshine, the women circled to eat slowly and deliberately, taking deep breaths for the first time since rising that morning. The tables under which I sat quietly among the crossed ankles of my mother and grandmother and aunts and listened to them talk.

Their voices, all of them thick with the country Southern accent I did not yet know was an accent, lifted and fell in waves of soft laughter, half-hearted complaint, honest inquiry, and communal instruction. Their conversation was punctuated with names of people, some of them familiar, others not, that I knew intuitively were my people—Minnie Lee. Annie Belle. Lessie Mae.

In the dimness, unable to sit up straight without hitting my head and rattling the dishes, I learned that a lady didn't say the word pregnant in public and, instead, referred to someone expecting a child as being "p.g." I learned that in-laws, at least in our family, stood on equal footing with everyone else. I learned that, in that time and place, being a woman meant eating last and enjoying the meal more.

And I learned how to tell stories. I learned which details to include and which ones won't be missed. I learned how to mimic the voices of the characters and where to throw in a "bless her heart" or "Lord, have mercy." I learned the value of an appreciative audience and the necessity of a powerful ending.

Underneath those tables, the ones without a single cloth napkin or lit candle, I felt the first stirring of an identity, the first inkling that words are powerful, that story is what connects us, that sharing can make us whole.

That is why I set the table. I make the sharpness of the knife blade and the curving lip of the bowl an offering. The lit candles become a prayer. I say to those who gather around it, "This is a place deserving of attention, deserving of time. The table is not just for holding food, but for holding us."

DECEMBER 10, 2017

Owen, my new dog, and I were out walking. At the crossroads, we saw two cars had pulled over. Two cars containing so many children that I wondered how they all fit. Clamoring over the deep ditch like clowns spilling out into the big top, they gathered along the edge of the cotton field yet-to-be-picked. A mother, still standing in the road, was aiming a 35mm camera at the clowns/children. "Grandma," she explained when she saw me and Owen, "would never forgive us if we didn't get a picture in the south Georgia snow."

I've never liked that phrase, south Georgia snow. It's always seemed just a little too cute. What my twelfth-grade English teacher Dorothy Brannen would have circled with her red pen and called trite. And it also makes me a little defensive, as though snow is such a wonderful thing that a land without it is backward, overly provincial, pitiful. But this morning—with the fog a thick and even blanket stretching all the way from treetop to heaven, one solid swath of pale gray enveloping and at the same time silhouetting the near leafless trees in the pecan grove—the field at the edge of the road did look as though it were covered in snow.

Which made me think about the Christmas Eve it snowed in Adabelle and the time it snowed at Wesleyan. And the weekend we went to Boone, North Carolina, to ski, only Kate had broken her pelvis when she fell off a horse, so while everybody else was flying down the mountain, she spent the weekend tromping through the snow on crutches and I tromped along behind her serving as ballast. I can still see our tracks in the snow—footprints and crutch marks.

That last memory makes me pause. I really can see the tracks, dark indentations in the crisp, cold white. Three ovals for the boots and two circles for the crutch tips. The ovals, the footprints, they make two lines, side by side but different.

I stop the memory reel. I rewind to make sure. My footprints make two lines. Kate's crutches make two more lines. Her single foot touching the ground makes one more line. Five lines through the snow.

Fourth grade. Big piece of dark blue construction paper. Create a snow scene, we were told. What did we south Georgia children know of snow?

I brushed thick white paint across the bottom of the paper and, while it dried, I put a few stars in the dark blue sky. I watched my classmates attempt to create realistic human figures on their winter landscapes. I knew my limitations. My scene would be people-less. Quiet, serene. A snowy hill adorned with just trees.

I decided to add some footprints. Black paint, small brush.

Two rows of tiny black ovals moving up the hill toward the sky. I remember thinking it was mysterious, that no one would ever know who made those footprints, where she was going, what she was doing out there in the snow, alone.

At about that moment, my teacher appeared, looking over my shoulder. "That's not how footprints look," she said condescendingly. "Footprints make one straight line." She walked away.

She was wrong. I knew it then in the way that a nine-year-old knows things she can't put into words. I knew it thirty years later when Kate and I trudged slowly over the mountain. And I know it now, with another twenty years' distance, sitting in my car gazing out over a field of south Georgia snow.

My footprints don't make a straight line. They weave and wobble. They turn in, then out. They crush things inadvertently and move on. They leave a record but don't always answer questions. Footprints, in the snow or otherwise, don't make a straight line.

DECEMBER 24, 2017

Chambless is five. Her future career goals include being a mermaid. At a recent Georgia Southern football game, she excitedly noted that all of the cheerleaders had golden hair—"just like me." She also knows and uses words like cornucopia.

Just the other day, she sneaked up from behind and saw her mother placing an Amazon order. It happened to be an order for a highly coveted Christmas gift. Alerted somehow to her precocious child, Jennifer quickly turned the situation to parental advantage and said, "Your dad and I were going to get you this for Christmas, but now that you have found out I guess we won't. If you still want it you will have to write a letter to Santa and ask him."

The letter was quickly written and dispatched, and shortly thereafter I received a request for the use of my very important Amazon Prime Two-Day Free Shipping account on behalf of Santa Claus. Click, click, done. The incident got me thinking back to when I was Chambless's age and my highly coveted Christmas present was a Ginny doll, a hard plastic doll with jointed limbs and the availability of an extensive wardrobe of fashionable clothes.

Several weeks before Christmas my mother sent me to get something for her from her bedroom.

I had already demonstrated at that point the personality traits that more benevolent friends and family now describe as diligence and organizational skills—and which would ultimately lead to my self-diagnosis of OCD—and when I could not find whatever the now-forgotten object was in whatever place Mama had indicated it would be found, I began searching in other places, intent on not disappointing her by saying I couldn't find it. Being a firstborn is hard.

Inside Mama and Daddy's bedroom closet was a cardboard box, nearly as tall as I, in which Mama, a child of the Depression, kept remnants. She never threw away any piece of fabric, convinced that one day they could be used. And, in fact, most of them eventually were when she and Grannie made a quilt for me. Having exhausted every other location, I began rummaging in the box.

About halfway down I came across not the object for which I had been searching but a Ginny doll. The realization of what the discovery meant was, I'm sure, both surprising and shocking, but I remember neither of those feelings, only the thought that I had to continue the search. When I finally located the object, I took it into the living room and presented it proudly to Mama, never saying a word about what else I had found.

I was an adult before I told anyone the story of how I came to know the truth about Christmas.

There is a song by John Lennon that begins with the lyric, "So, this is Christmas." It always strikes me as wistful and just short of cynical but also a little too true, and I listen to it every year as a reminder that part of my celebration of this holy season has to include an examination of that truth, that if the season is to mean anything at all we must acknowledge the reality, not just the ideal.

Which includes the fact that not every highly coveted gift is received, that sometimes we wish and hope and maybe even pray for something we don't get, we can't have.

Yet it also means that, once we learn that immutable fact, we tend to learn another, complementary one: that the central idea behind the season is not the gift-receiving, but the gift-giving. Which is why we adults go to such elaborate means—including facilitating letters to Santa and utilizing Amazon Prime—to see children be delighted by what they find under the tree.

And which is why—even in places ravaged by hurricanes and floods, in places where landmines are easier to find than Christmas lights, in places where most five-year-olds know nothing of cornucopias and the plenty they represent—mothers and fathers, grandmothers and grandfathers, doting aunts and uncles still wait with anticipation, with hope, with hunger for the brief respite afforded by the joy reflected on their children's faces Christmas morning.

I never told my parents that I no longer believed. That would have been a lie.

"*In this universe we are given two gifts: the ability to love, and the ability to ask questions. Which are, at the same time, the fires that warm us and the fires that scorch us.*"

—Mary Oliver, *Upstream*

JANUARY 7, 2018

"Watch for deer."

It is an admonition that—along with "Be sweet" and "Tell your mama and them hey"—is a mandatory component of the standard ritual of the south Georgia goodbye. I don't remember too many times in my life in which I have taken leave of someplace that I did not receive one, two, or all three of them. My required response, the response of anyone departing, is the simple "I will." It reminds me a lot of the marriage vow.

Several years ago I had been to Nahunta to the funeral home visitation for the grandmother of two of my dearest friends. It was dark and late, and the way home was two hours on two-lane highways. I made my way around the funeral home bidding all the various loved ones good night and assuring them that I'd be back the next morning for the service, and, to a person, every single one of them said, "Watch for deer."

And I did. All the way back up Highway 301 through Jesup and Ludowici and Glennville and Claxton and all the way to my driveway. I was within a few yards of the carport when I heard a boom and felt a rattle that, to one schooled in such things, was instantly recognizable as the sound of a grown deer running headlong into an SUV.

The deer, mercifully, died and I, fortunately, had excellent insurance coverage. Done and done. Except that now every time someone tells me to watch for deer and every time I turn into my driveway late at night, I get a little jolt of adrenaline, half expecting another encounter with something racing through the dark.

Walking around outside in the dark has, over the past year or so, become one of my favorite things to do. It is something to which I look forward, an activity that produces inspiration rather than requiring it. It is a daily comfort, a dependable solace, a soothing balm. And, until just the other night, it never occurred to me to watch for deer.

I often hear them rustling in the branch or get a glimpse of them leaping along the horizon under the light of a full moon, but those deer, the rustling and leaping deer, are disembodied, ethereal, practically magical. They are not the same as the deer about which I have been warned, for which I must always be on alert, of which I must force myself to have some fear.

One night a couple of weeks ago Owen and I were walking the perimeter of the yard, just along the back line where the saw-tooth oaks and the sycamore grow, when suddenly, with only the faintest rustling of fallen limbs and dried grass, a deer came running at full speed directly across our path, no more than twenty-five feet in front of us. I stopped hard and focused as best I could in the pale yellow cone of the yard light.

I could make out the curve of antlers resting like a crown on his head. His white belly flashed like a semaphore with each jump. He was about as tall as I am, hoof to tip. And in two, maybe three seconds he was gone—across the driveway, into the field.

I was surprised that Owen didn't chase him. Instead, the two of us stood very still staring toward the spot where the deer had disappeared into the darkness as I realized he'd followed the same route as the deer who had hit me three years ago. The exact same route. It was as though there was a ley line cutting through the backyard.

All through Christmas and on to New Year's, as the weather got colder and the moon grew larger, Owen and I walked. And I kept thinking about the deer, both of them. It was as though I'd been handed a knot to unravel, a code to break. Then, just as the moon reached full, an egg yolk threatening to break, I figured it out.

"Watch for deer" was more than an encouragement of safe

driving. More than a reminder toward diligence. Every time my grandmother, my mother, my friends had said "Watch for deer," it had meant far more than just "Be careful." It had meant and would always mean "Pay attention. There is more happening here than you can see."

Watch for deer and you may find yourself face to face with wildness. Watch for deer and you may realize how little there is to fear. Watch for deer and you just may find magic humming through the ground beneath your feet.

JANUARY 21, 2018

What now?

The string of holidays tumbling one right after the other like puppies down a hill is over. The unexpected magic of a new year snowfall has melted and left behind thousands of digital photos, but little else. The joie de football created by high hopes and provincialism has faded with the disappointing scores.

So what now? What is going to keep me alive through the dead of winter—when the last dangling hydrangea leaves are slimy and brown, when the rain has left ruts dried into deep ditches and hard shards of clay that crunch beneath my feet like glass, when the wind rattles the trees, the windows, and even my bones?

There is not much I like about this season. Homemade soup, Russian tea, high school basketball. That's about it. I am not much of one for the whole curling up with a book and a blanket thing or the curling up with Netflix and a blanket thing or, really, curling up at all. It gives me a headache to hunch my shoulders, to curve my spine.

So, instead of turning up the heat and closing the shades, opening a bag of Oreos, and grabbing the remote control, I go outside. Make myself go outside. Force myself to face down the chill and the wind. I turn myself into a clothing lasagna. Cuddl Duds and tights and socks, more Cuddl Duds and undershirt and sweatshirt, coat and gloves and earmuffs. I cross the threshold, cross the porch, and walk.

Into the wind and away from the place where the sun is setting in bleached-out colors, I don't see much worth noting. There is no animal movement. Not even the birds. The fields are all cut over. The landscape is one wide swath of beige.

What now? The familiar, nagging question returns, an uninvited companion, and I have no idea to whom I am directing the inquiry—Myself? God? The trees that arc over my head like flying buttresses? I do know it is not just a New Year's resolution-type question. I do know that it's not about the next hour or day or week. I know that what I am asking has nothing to do with what is written on my calendar and everything to do with what is written on my heart.

And what might that be? If I believe all the Bible verses given to me for memorization by Sunday school teachers over the years, there is a great deal of Scripture written there, but I suspect there is something more, something written in my own hand. If I am to move through this cold and dark season with any purpose, any hope of survival, I have to know what it says.

Behind me the sun has set quickly, the pale lavender sky melting like butter on toast. Movement is keeping me warmer than I'd have thought when I started out, but my toes are beginning to tingle. The interminable stream of interrogatory sentences is beginning to slow, along with my breath. Time to go home.

Unpeeled of all the layers, I walk through the house looking at my phone. I notice a friend's new Facebook profile photo in which he is sporting a sweatshirt from his alma mater. There is something disorienting about it. Something odd about this face I know so well. It takes me a moment to realize that the photo was taken in a mirror and "Georgia" is written backwards across his chest. Readable, but disorienting.

I pause and close my eyes, aware suddenly that there is a discovery to be had somewhere amid the pixels and computer code. Could it be that I have just been disoriented, like a hiker caught in an avalanche? That what is written on my heart, the instructions that are meant to get me from here to there, are still readable and still the same as they have always been? That I can trust my ability to see what is true despite its appearing to be the mirror opposite?

Eyes open, I look around. There is a wall of books. There is a painting of the marsh on Saint Simons. There is a photo of me holding my great-nephew on the day of his baptism. With every turn of my head the answer grows clearer.

What now? Only what is already here. Only this. This breath. This moment. This life.

FEBRUARY 4, 2018

I was only six when my family moved from Mikell Street, and yet it remains, all these years later, my neighborhood. And the people who lived on that street and the one behind it, College Lane, remain, all these years later, my people. So I don't suppose that the sadness that rose up in me when I heard the news of the death of one of my early playmates should have been totally unexpected. But it was.

There was a gang of us in the neighborhood. A dozen or so at the core—the Campbells, the Keys, the Morrisses, my brother, my cousins, and I—who rambled up and down the streets and into and out of each other's yards with a freedom I cannot even imagine for the four- and five-year-olds I know today. We raced our broomstick ponies and played tea party and sat on quilts to eat each other's birthday cakes. The clotheslines that festooned our backyards with white sheet flags and towel semaphores may have been the boundaries for land lots, but to us they were nothing more than base in our endless games of chase.

I locked arms with Debra and Dianne to form an impenetrable bond in Red Rover. I bent to hurry under the London Bridge built by Cathy and Glenda. I joined hands with everybody in Ring Around the Rosie to make a circle with no beginning and no ending. We taught each other how to follow rules, how to play fair, how to make sure everybody got included. We taught each other confidence and security and community.

My family lived at one end of the block, and on the other end was Mr. Newton's store, a narrow cement block building painted an avocado green color, to which I was allowed to take my brother by one hand and walk all by myself, two nickels clutched in the other hand. With those two nickels I would buy cookies from the big glass jar with the bright red top or a handful of Squirrel Nuts and Mary Janes that Mr. Newton would drop into a tiny brown paper bag. I can still see with great clarity the wooden floor, its shine long gone, scuffed away by years of neighborhood dwellers shuffling their way in for a loaf of Sunbeam bread stacked on the wire shelves near the door or a bottle of Coca-Cola from the long red cooler.

The Campbells lived about halfway between our house and Mr. Newton's store. Mama and Miss Bonnie were great friends. They were both fine seamstresses and could talk to each other forever, it seemed, about fabric and patterns and notions, a fact that allowed for a bit more perceived freedom for my brother Keith and I and Miss Bonnie and Mr. Pete's children, Phil and Ann.

One overcast Saturday afternoon I was at the Campbells' house to play with Ann and Miss Bonnie decided to make cookies. Miss Bonnie had the first stove I'd ever seen with glass in the door, and Ann and I were just tall enough to press our faces up to the glass and watch the cookies rise in the amber light of the oven. It was like being a witness to magic.

I have absolutely no memory of the taste of those cookies, but the image of them rising slowly, the heat hovering like a mirage, my friend and I mesmerized by them in the safety and obliviousness of childhood remains clear and true all these decades later.

So no, I don't suppose I should be surprised that seeing Ann's obituary would trigger a wave of sadness and a waterfall of memories. That the customary string of words and dates and names that are supposed to sum up a life would leave me bewildered and unable to do simple math in my head. That the day's ordinary noise and activity would fade away as I sat for a while inside my five-year-old self.

I had not seen Ann in years and I couldn't say that I knew much about her life as an adult. She had married, had children. She was a grandmother. And a widow. I read the names of the people left to mourn her passing, the ones I know and the ones I don't. I tried to get a picture of my childhood friend—the little blonde girl who was quiet and easy among so many of us who were anything but—as a grown woman. It must have been the third time through that I saw it: "Most of her life," the obituary read, "Ann was a homemaker."

And there I was, back on Mikell Street again. Back with the Campbells, the Keys, the Morrisses, my brother, and my cousins. Back home. And back with the people who made it home and made those homes. The mothers and fathers, the neighbors and Mr. Newton, all the adults who created a place where children felt safe without even knowing it, where children learned to be adults by watching the good ones around them.

FEBRUARY 18, 2018

Owen is teaching me a lot. It is, of course, in his job description. A person doesn't take on the responsibility of a puppy without also accepting the unavoidable stretching, even breaking of one's parameters. I knew this when, on Halloween afternoon, I arrived at home to find him, who had never been seen before, sitting under the carport with an expression on his face that could be read as either "Where have you been? I've been so worried" or "Where have you been? I can't believe you kept me waiting."

What I didn't know was that the elements of the Owen curriculum would be so vastly different from those of my previous two dogs, the regal and loyal Ginny and the grateful and placid Lily.

He is teaching me, for example, to look for launching pads.

Owen is, as it turns out, a jumper. He never takes the steps, using them instead as the springboard from which he throws himself into a replication of Mary Lou Retton mid-vault and sailing over them a good four feet to land with grace that would move even the Russian judge to award him a 10.0. He turns butterfly-chasing into ballet, leaping into the air in tour jetés to rival Baryshnikov's, and his favorite parts of the dirt road are the places where the woods on either side are high enough that he can hurl himself over the edge and cross the ditch to land somewhere close to my feet.

Sometimes he rolls, sometimes he face-plants, but always he gets back up and leaps again. He is teaching me that the ground is always going to be there. Always. He is teaching me that I will never jump and be lost forever in oblivion, that however far the fall there will always be something on which I can, however awkwardly, regain my footing.

He is also, through his favorite toy, teaching me something about the joy of struggle.

That toy is the long, knotted rope that I throw and he retrieves, that I throw again and he retrieves again, that I throw again and again and again and he retrieves again and again and again. Until, that is, the moment when he decides that tug-of-war would be more fun than fetch. The moment when he clamps his teeth down onto the knot and refuses to release it. The moment when I realize that I'm trying and failing in getting the toy out of his mouth. The moment when I start wondering why I don't just let go.

Because, let's be honest, that is always the first thought. When the effort becomes struggle, the work becomes combat, the attempt becomes conflict, it is always the easiest, quickest, simplest thing to do. Let go. Walk away. Give up.

My niece Kate works for a nonprofit foundation that recently received a large grant, a grant big enough to do a lot of good for its constituency. She shared with me a part of the letter notifying them of the award and encouraging them in what is not going to be an easy endeavor. "Remember," the letter read, "you were made for this struggle."

I read it through twice, three times, as tears sprang to my eyes. Could that be true? If it is—and there was something in me that said it is—then letting go, walking away, and giving up couldn't be the only options when the battle engages, when fatigue sets in, when life gets harder than I ever imagined it could.

I think about me and Owen in the front yard, on either end of the rope toy. Me grimacing and yanking and sighing with frustration. Him growling and jerking and drooling with joy. With every pull he is trying to take me to a place of playfulness and engagement, trying to get me to see that this, too, is a game. Just a different one. With different rules. And different expectations. If I let go, both games are over. If I hold on, I may yet have fun.

If I hold on, I may find that I am stronger than I ever thought I could be. If I stay, I may find that the view changes with the season. And if I don't give up, I may find that not only was I made for this struggle, but this struggle was made for me.

MARCH 4, 2018

Memory is a funny thing. This is how it works. Or, more accurately, this is how mine works:

I brush my teeth twice a day. And every time I pick up my toothbrush—every single time—I think about my friend Jim.

Jim was a student in the first class I taught as an adjunct professor at Georgia Southern University. He sat on the front row, against the wall of the mobile unit that had been constructed close enough to the baseball field that, during those warm spring evenings when we met to talk about business law, we could hear the crowds at the baseball stadium roar with enthusiasm when the home team made a great defensive play or hit a homerun.

Jim had been in the Marines before coming to school, so he was older than most of the other students. Not by much, but enough. He'd been to war, real war, and, as I would learn later when he came to work for me and became my friend, real war had made its mark.

After he graduated from Georgia Southern, he got his MBA at the University of Georgia and accepted a job with Johnson & Johnson, the company that makes baby powder and baby shampoo and baby lotion, Band-Aids and Benadryl and Tylenol. At the time they also made Reach toothbrushes, and on one of my visits Jim presented me with a plastic bagful. Assuming that I followed recommended protocol and changed my toothbrush every three months, that bag lasted about four years.

Four years during which Jim changed jobs a couple of times. During which he and I took a trip to New York City—saw the Braves play the Mets at Shea Stadium, ate brunch at Tavern on the Green, hiked all over Central Park, and had a stranger take our photo on top of the Empire State Building. During which the demons with which he had struggled for years tightened their grip on his will and his soul.

It's been over twenty years since Jim and I became friends, over fifteen since he gave me the toothbrushes, over four now since he died.

Yesterday I was at Walmart looking at toothbrushes, marveling at the vast array of colors and handles and bristles. I was uncharacteristically indecisive. "It shouldn't be this difficult," I offered to the woman standing beside me and also staring blankly at the singles, the doubles, the four-packs, "to pick out a toothbrush."

I finally decided, based—I have to admit—more on color than on claimed efficacy of tartar removal, and last night, as I squeezed the toothpaste onto its stiff new bristles, I remembered Jim. As I always do.

I know more about Alzheimer's than I ever wanted to know. I have watched it steal the minds of the two women who loved me most, and I have learned in the watching that the connections the brain sometimes makes between totally unrelated objects can be simultaneously uproariously funny and heartbreakingly sad. What I have concluded, however, is that no matter how jolting and disconcerting it might be to me to hear a dog referred to as a chair, there is, to the speaker at least, always some rationale, some logic behind the misspoken word, the confused syllables, the misaligned sounds.

And on the basis of that conclusion, I have further decided that if I, as a result of genetics or too much aspartame or any other vile attacker, succumb to Alzheimer's at some point in the future, I will most likely refer to my toothbrush as Jim. No one should be concerned. I will know what I'm doing. I'll be remembering.

MARCH 18, 2018

They dragged the ditches a few weeks ago. They hauled their big, noisy, mustard yellow machines out to my edge of the county, the imaginary line separating Bulloch County from Evans, and set about scooping every imaginable form of detritus from the long, open graves. Once exhumed, the roots and rocks, broken bottles and aluminum cans, plastic bags with faded logos, were tossed into—and left in—the middle of the road.

I am not complaining. The cost-benefit analysis that one constantly makes or finds being made on one's behalf when one chooses to live in the country makes it pretty clear that, between the two choices, dragging the ditches is the lesser of two evils.

One option is to allow the ditches to slowly fill with the leaves and vines and fallen branches, a choice that will eventually result in leaving the rain nowhere to drain, no way to reach the creek, creating what I like to think of as a combination of Mr. Toad's Wild Ride and the Log Jamboree without the expense of a trip to Orlando or Six Flags. The other option is the aforementioned dragging, which leaves the road temporarily lumpy and littered with hazards that, not avoided, can puncture a tire or knock off a muffler and feeling like—to continue with the theme park metaphor—something akin to the Dahlonega Mine Train.

And so the ditches got dragged.

It was a beautiful afternoon, one of those seventy-degree days that made us think Gen. Beauregard Lee had, at long last, entered his dotage and couldn't tell his shadow from a hole in the ground, and Owen and I had ventured well over a mile from home. He kept running on ahead and I kept stopping to examine the items that had been left in our path. The road turned into a veritable archaeological dig—branches longer than my leg and bigger around, with jagged ends that testified to the storms that had ripped them from their trees; plastic bottles and beer cans; and big chunks of concrete, the size of a tabletop.

For a moment, recalling a vague image from HGTV of a walkway made of salvage concrete, I considered borrowing Daddy's truck to haul it home. It would not be the craziest thing for which I've borrowed his truck, but I released the idea as I remembered the number of loads of pea gravel that cute couple from Mississippi had needed to finish their project. Still, I moved the biggest pieces to the sides of the road, out of the middle where they'd been left to become hazards to cars and trucks and four-wheelers.

The idea I didn't release, though, the one that followed me home and stuck around, was the idea that roads aren't the only things that need the occasional ditch-dragging, the every-once-in-a-while digging up and tossing aside.

I went to visit some friends the other day. It wasn't a long visit; it didn't have to be. We ate well, we laughed, and we dragged some ditches. Talked about some things that, over time, have accumulated in dark and damp piles, things that have clogged the water flow. We just threw those things into the middle of the road, the road we still had to walk, and took good long looks at them to decide which ones were harmless enough to leave where they were and which ones needed to be moved.

Because there are some logs, some pieces of concrete that are just too dangerous to leave where they are. Logs like resentment. Chunks of concrete like unforgiveness. In distraction and hurry we ignore the danger and find out only after the tire goes flat or the relationship disintegrates that the destruction could have been avoided if only we had cleared the road.

APRIL 1, 2018

The lethargy of spring and the lingering weight of pollen in my head and chest have left me, this year, all too comfortable with the vocabulary of Lent. The wind wails across the still-empty fields and I watch with bone-heavy fatigue twisting cones of dust, the dust from which I've come and to which I will return. It seems years ago that I stood at the altar and voluntarily accepted the ashes. I didn't think it would last this long.

But it has. And the burden that greets me each morning is not just the cold but the weariness of impotence and resignation. The reminder that on the same day Valentine's candy collided with ashes, they were both overlapped by a murderous tragedy in an otherwise ordinary high school. An event that has shadowed every single day of the season in which I and my fellow Christians find ourselves called to repentance.

For eighteen years I have given my professional self to the job of prosecuting juvenile offenders in the place I have called home for my entire life. It is a job that forces me to make hard decisions, to ask hard questions, to sometimes disregard the pleas of well-meaning parents. It requires me to take the long view, to look at today's behavior in light of tomorrow, to utilize whatever resources are available, in the words of the Juvenile Code, to secure "the moral, emotional, mental, and physical welfare" of the children whose lives intersect mine.

It is not easy.

That is not a request for sympathy or affirmation. It is simply a fact. And, in light of a recent spate of incidents in our own communities in which our children have engaged in making threats against each other and their schools, I have to stop to wonder—not for the first or the second or the hundredth time—

what is going on here. Why are children threatening to kill other children? Why are they threatening to blow up their schools? Why are they posting hate-filled racial epithets on social media and then acting perplexed when consequences result?

The answer, I think, is one of two things. Either the child has become absolutely numb to words because of the way culture has appropriated hate speech and profanity as "art," or he lives in an environment where that kind of language is the norm, where the adults in his life suffer from a poverty so great that their only power comes from hating, criticizing, and looking down on others.

What that means is that we—the adults who are birthing and rearing and modeling for these children—have failed to teach them the power of words. Whether we have forgotten or chosen to ignore that words are the original creator, we can no longer pretend it doesn't matter.

So now it is time to repent. Time to put off the sackcloth and ashes, time to rise from the heap of sorrow and anger and despair, time to stride into the authority that is ours by virtue of having listened to the stories, lived through the struggles, learned what the long view means. Time to stop giving ourselves a pass for the occasional racist or sexist or homophobic remark because we know that we're basically good people. Time to start using words—every single word—in a thoughtful and respectful way.

And when we do, spring will come. New things will grow. Resurrection will be ours.

APRIL 15, 2018

Late last night, fueled by the residual adrenaline of a hectic court day and the leftover caffeine from a combination of migraine medicine and sweet tea at supper, I went outside to walk around for a while. There is nothing like darkness, nature's darkness broken only by distant starlight, to remind a person of her smallness and the smallness of the things and thoughts that cultivate discontent.

I moved away from the beams cast by the floodlights, splayed out across the yard in the shape of giant megaphones, being careful not to step in one of the holes that Owen has dug in the front yard, and made my way toward the edge of the field that will soon be planted with cotton seed. The evening damp settled on my hands and cheeks, and in the distance I heard the dull hum that is the relentless rush of traffic on the interstate.

In the absence of clouds, the stars were bright enough to create shadows—the light pole a long smudge across my driveway, the places where my brother had turned the tractor wavy lines—and I tilted my head to find the Big Dipper. It is the only constellation I can ever find with any consistency, any accuracy. Locating the large ladle in the endless sky is like placing a pushpin on a map. You are here.

But the Big Dipper is not what I saw. What I saw was Orion. Clear as day. Exactly like a textbook photo.

It's funny what happens when you see something you don't expect to see. Something you've never seen before. Something you've never been able to see before. What happens is that you doubt yourself, your vision. You shake your head and blink your eyes and, when mere blinking doesn't change what you see, you close them and you count to ten and look again.

And when it's still Orion dangling there in the southwest sky, you take a deep breath and stare in amazement. Motionless, silent amazement.

I don't know how long I stared. How long I stood in the darkness looking up at the light. How long I held my arms around my chest as though to hold in a heart that might explode with astonishment at any moment.

It's funny what happens when you see something you have never seen before. What happens when you choose to believe yourself, your vision. You want to see more, know more.

So this morning I went searching. I found that while it was the Greeks who gave the constellation the name Orion, meaning "the hunter," the Babylonians called it "the heavenly shepherd." The three stars that are generally described as Orion's belt are known as The Three Marys in Spain and Latin America, and the Lakota Native Americans call it Tayamnicankhu, the spine of a bison. In some Hungarian traditions, it is known as a "judge's stick." I smiled when I read that, imagining the judges before whom I appear wielding a stick rather than a gavel.

I have a couple of theories as to why I was suddenly able to see Orion when I never had before. The first one has to do with a change in my contact lenses. That theory is a lot less fun than the second, which is that magic still exists and occasionally the necessary ingredients—in this case a cool clear night, caffeine, and a woman with a vivid imagination and an affinity for mystery—come together to cast a spell of enchantment.

I like the latter. And I like to think that those ingredients are close at hand all the time. That they are available to all of us. Everywhere. That all we must do is walk outside.

APRIL 29, 2018

There are some stories you don't tell. Ever. Not to anyone. There are some stories you tell all the time, over and over, with such panache and aplomb that you know exactly the moment when the audience will gasp or nod or cover its mouth in the impossible attempt to stifle the inappropriate laugh.

And there are some stories you tell, but only rarely. Only when the time is right. When that part of your heart where the most precious things are locked away whispers, "Now." This is one of those stories.

I was back at Wesleyan last weekend for my fortieth reunion. About thirty of my classmates joined me. We took a lot of photos, gave and received a lot of hugs, and wore a lot of purple. We talked about the people who weren't there and gave them heck in absentia. We did a lot of remembering.

It was from that remembering, that neurological pump primed by the smiles and laughs that look and sound absolutely no different from the ones I last saw and heard in 1978, that the story rose to the surface like the witches we used to say rose from Foster Lake on Halloween to free the students from class.

It is the story of a bright but naive seventeen-year-old who visited Wesleyan for a scholarship weekend and went home and told her parents, "I'm going there." The one who didn't apply to any other college, so sure was she that somehow, some way Wesleyan would be where she would end up. It's the story of the girl who was so excited to have seen that optimism rewarded that she wandered around the first week introducing herself to so many people that someone mistook her for a faculty member.

And it's the story of the girl who, having endured—and at the same time somehow enjoyed—the juvenile initiation rites inflicted on her and her classmates by the upperclassmen, found a spot on the grass, far away from the drone of conversation in the dorm, to sit under the honey drip of the setting sun and marvel at her incredible good fortune.

Most of my friends from high school were, at that exact moment, living the vastly different experience of sorority rush. I didn't know much about the string of invitations and parties beyond the fact that it involved the process of, ultimately, being chosen. Sitting there with my knees pulled up to my chest, looking out over the campus as the street lamps began to come on, I was struck forcefully by what was probably the first truly adult thought I'd ever had, the thought that what I had just been through—the ridiculous outfit included—was quite the opposite of being chosen and was, in fact, the culmination of my choosing.

Choosing and being chosen, it was clear, are quite different things. And for this bright but naive—and did I mention insecure?—seventeen-year-old it was more than different. It was critical. I would never have had the self-confidence, the assurance, the courage to say, "Pick me." I would never have believed that anyone would.

But I did have the self-confidence and assurance and courage to trust my choice. I did know, from the moment I dragged my trunk into the dorm room I would share with Kim from Titusville, Florida, that I had found my home. And I have trusted it every moment since.

On Saturday night, a couple of hundred yards and nearly forty-four years away from that spot of grass, on a patio lit only by paper bag luminaries, we sat—my Wesleyan sisters and I. We talked about the people we loved then and the ones we still do. We filled in the gaps in each other's stories, moving around the patio from one cluster to another, a waltz without accompaniment. We listened and nodded and gave each other permission to be those girls again, the ones who chose.

It was chilly for late April. At one point a few drops of rain fell on our heads like a christening. And, too soon, it was time to go.

Of all the decisions I have ever made, the one that took me there, that keeps me there even now is the only one that I have never second-guessed. Perhaps I was not as naive, as insecure as I thought. Or perhaps I was simply, even then, listening to my heart say, "Now."

MAY 13, 2018

It is spring. It is Saturday afternoon. The sun that slants through the living room window is more than enough light for me to do the close and tedious work of replacing a hem that has come undone in one of my favorite dresses. It has unraveled like the string at the top of Owen's dog food bag, and I am just a little exasperated that I have to take even a few minutes of this gloriously warm and bright day to correct the shoddy workmanship of whoever it was who put in these stitches, obviously by machine, not hand.

The sewing basket from which I take the needle and thread was my mother's for many years and she gave it to me, freshly lined with new velvet and satin, when I first learned to sew. It was something like a father passing on his hunting rifle, a recognition that I'd gained enough skill at something that was important to her to be acknowledged and encouraged.

When I was growing up, Mama supplemented our family income by—as we used to say—taking in sewing. Day after day, night after night, our kitchen table was draped with fabric, the smell of dye drifting through the house as thick as the scent of pot roast on Sunday. She pinned crinkly, tissue-thin pattern pieces to the cloth like jigsaw pieces with barely an inch between them, so frugal with the fabric that she always needed at least a quarter yard less than the pattern envelope indicated. She cut around these pieces with heavy metal scissors that we were not allowed to use for anything else. And then she sat down to the brown Singer, whose rhythmic rattle lulled me to sleep on many a summer night as its song drifted in and out of the open windows of our house, and stitched those separate pieces together into a single garment.

When I was ten or twelve, about the time that the sewing

basket was passed on, I took on the role of assistant. My job was to steam press the seams of bodices attached to skirts, of fronts attached to backs, of sleeves attached to shoulders, to make sure that each one lay flat and even before it went back under the presser foot of the sewing machine to be sewn to the next piece. I can still feel the heft of the iron in my hand, the feel of the steam escaping from the top, the sizzle of the water as I refilled the port.

Handwork came later. Only after Mama had watched me press seams for a long time did she trust me with the simple but tedious task for which she was well known. Her instructions were specific: Make a double knot so that it will not pull through the fabric, but do not double the thread. A single strand is all you need for the handwork of putting in hems, tacking down facings. Take short, flat stitches. Make sure that they are invisible from the front. This is accomplished by catching a single thread of the fabric with the needle, feeding it through gently. When you are done, if you have done it all correctly, there will be no sign of the needle or the thread. This is the mark of a master seamstress—that there are no marks.

The instructions were more than instructions. They were a mantra, one that is stored not just in my memory but in my hands. I knot the thread, take up the dress with the fallen hem, and begin.

What I know now that I couldn't have known when I was twelve is that the confidence Mama showed in handing me that first dress and saying, "Here. Hem this," wasn't confidence in my ability. It was confidence in hers. Her ability to teach, to model, to show.

It is no small thing to trust. No small thing to hand over something of value—your money, your reputation, your heart—to another human being and say, "Here. Take care of this." It is always an all-or-nothing gamble. Because the one you have to trust is yourself.

MAY 27, 2018

"Long distance is the next best thing to being there." That was the advertising slogan of AT&T back when AT&T ruled the telecommunications industry, back when telephones had cords, back when it cost extra to call someone outside your area code. It was also the phrase that my Aunt June repeated over and over again to Grannie as I prepared to leave home for college and go a full 120 miles away. In Grannie's mind, however, next best was only slightly better than worst. Grannie wanted to see my face, hold my hands in hers.

I understand. I generally avoid telephone conversations lasting longer than five minutes. If the purpose of the call is to pass on information, five minutes is a gracious plenty. For anything else, a visit is warranted. Not always possible, but warranted. People need to see each other's faces. People need to hold each other's hands.

Tonight, though, I am willing to break my rule.

I walk out onto the porch, cell phone pressed to my ear. It has been raining off and on for days, and the cloud cover that stretches from one horizon to the other makes the cell reception inside the house, spotty under the best of circumstances, particularly treacherous. Outside, under the sky, the dampness of the night falling lightly on me like a veil, I will hear better. I will listen better. Ignoring the rocking chairs, I sit down at the edge of the porch, my back straight against one of the columns.

The voice on the other end of the line—though it's not a line anymore, if it ever really was—is one I know well. I would recognize it anywhere. It is a voice I know at every volume, in every cadence, with every inflection. It is a voice that carries with it more than just words. It is heavy with history.

There is no news to speak of, nothing momentous to share. It is not that kind of phone call. It is an "I just wanted to hear your voice" phone call. It is a "Remind me that these things are still true" phone call.

So we just talk. Run-on sentences. Phrases without objects. Subjects without verbs. We interrupt. We talk over each other. We pause to breathe. We laugh, we sigh, I—at least—swallow tears.

In 1977 two Voyager spacecraft were launched. Neither of the two had any particular destination. If any "advanced space-faring civilizations," as Carl Sagan called them, encounter either Voyager I or II—Voyager I should pass within about 1.6 light years of the star Gliese 445 in about 40,000 years—they will find on board the so-called Golden Records. Included among all the amazing sounds gathered to represent our planet—the sounds of whale songs and the Brandenburg Concerto, the sounds of volcanoes and earthquakes and thunder, the sounds of footsteps, the sound of a kiss—are voices. Human voices making greetings in fifty-five ancient and modern languages, human voices offered as, in the words of President Jimmy Carter, "a present from a small, distant world, a token...of our thoughts and feelings. We are attempting to survive our time so we may live into yours."

Voices as a present. A gift. An offering.

It fills me with amazement. Amazement that a combination of plastic and metal and the imagination that came up with binary code is, this very moment, allowing me to make that gift, to receive that gift from another human being, to be connected in a way that is even better than seeing his face, holding his hand. Amazement that the waxing moon, made invisible by the thick gray clouds, is still illuminating my front yard so well that I can make out fencerows and power lines and my mailbox at the edge of the road. Amazement that Grannie and AT&T may have both been wrong, that long distance may well—sometimes, at least— be better than being there.

JUNE 10, 2018

Three-plus miles. Eighty-plus degrees. Hot and sweaty in the best possible way. Home to a shower of lavender and well water.

It is almost sunset and, cleanliness aside, I can't resist the urge to go back outside, to squeeze an ounce or two more out of this day that is just a little longer than the day before, this day that is teasing me toward summer. The breeze is beginning to pick up in the branch. It ripples through the leaves in the top of the sycamore tree like an old man ruffling his grandson's hair.

The scent of soap, the angle of the sun, the riff of air across my bare arms ignite a Roman candle of memories. Long day in the front yard with cousins, dirt and grass stains washed away in a bathtub tinctured with Tide to ward off impetigo, front porch in pajamas listening to the grown-ups tell stories. Long day at church camp, little kid smells washed away by water so cold it makes you dance, church service followed by a trip to the concession stand for Milk Duds and a strange concoction of Coke and grape and orange Fanta we called a Suicide. Long day at the beach, sand and sweat washed away by sulfur-scented water from a rusty showerhead, barefoot stroll under a full moon.

I stand still for a moment. Let the memories wash over me. Like the water in the bathtub, the water from the showerhead, the waves of the ocean. I am encapsulated in water and memory. In time.

I was eight years old when I first experienced anticipation. First understood what it meant to know that something pleasurable was coming and feel the emotion ahead of time.

Fourth grade at Mattie Lively. My teacher, Elizabeth Curlin, had made a bulletin board for the month of May that consisted of one single daisy. The center was the size of a steering wheel and it had thirty-one petals, each one numbered and attached to the center by a single staple. First thing every morning, the petal corresponding to that day on the calendar was plucked off by a lucky student chosen by Mrs. Curlin.

As the month progressed the daisy grew more and more pitiful. We, conversely, grew more and more enthusiastic. The approach of summer, with its promise of Popsicles, Push Ups, and playing under the water hose, made even the best-behaved of us loud and rambunctious. Anticipation is a powerful drug.

And in the stillness, I feel it rising even now. Anticipation.

I am tasting tomatoes that have not yet appeared on the vine and sweet corn that has not yet appeared on the stalk. I am watching my legs and arms turn a warmer shade of pink. I am hearing waves crash so loudly that conversation is impossible.

Across the field the sun has stained the sky bright pink, deep violet. It is trembling in those last few moments before it disappears for the night. Tomorrow it will stay a little longer. Tomorrow summer will be one day closer. I can hardly wait.

JUNE 24, 2018

There is still enough light in the sky to make out clouds. They are mauve and smoky violet, muted lavender and the palest of grays. One looks like a dolphin caught in mid-leap. Another like a giant Mickey Mouse hand.

Across the way, toward town, a single streak of lightning makes a rip through the sky—heaven to horizon, orange-red like Mercurochrome. Heat lightning or the other kind, I can't tell. It is certainly hot enough for heat lightning; it feels as though I am wearing the air itself. On the other hand, the radar app on my phone is flashing an alert. More rain on the way.

The grass is between cuttings. It has grown quickly under the encouragement of daily showers, and its too-tall blades slap at my ankles. It reminds me that when things are watered they grow.

Not just plants. Everything. Tangible and non.

I listen to a lot of podcasts. It is the method I have adopted for curating the information I absorb from the world, a deliberate attempt to keep out the voices that are so loud I can't hear what they are saying. I like the sense of autonomy, however false it may be, that it gives me, the idea that I can decide what topics are important and about which I want to know more, the idea that these thoughtful, articulate people are waiting to engage me in a conversation of sorts.

One of the podcasts that I occasionally download is called "The One You Feed." The host begins each interview by retelling the Native American story in which a grandfather tells his grandson that a good wolf and an evil wolf reside in each person. When the grandson asks which one prevails, the grandfather responds, "The one you feed."

After you've heard the story three or four times it loses some of its potency. Maybe that's why I haven't listened to that podcast in a while. But tonight, in light of my itchy ankles, I find myself reconsidering its hard-sell message.

We are always feeding, watering something. Attitudes, relationships, opinions. Dreams, theories, priorities. And they will grow, like grass or wolves, in direct response to what they are fed, how often they are watered.

The sky has lost its purpleness now. It has faded into tarnished silver. The clouds are flat and nearly invisible. They hide what little moon, what few stars might otherwise offer a little light to my perambulation. I'm walking by memory mostly. I know the rise and fall of a yard that used to be a field and, twenty-five years later, still bears the indentations of a plow.

One field away is the house my parents built, the one into which we moved when I was still in high school and would have thought that moving to the farm was the worst thing that had ever happened to me had I not been counting down the days until

I would leave for college. It reminds me that what we feed and water doesn't just influence us, but those to whom we are connected as well.

I am here, under this stretch of sky at this moment, because when he was thirty-eight years old my father decided to feed the longing in his heart to return to the land. And because twenty years before that he went to church in the tiny community of Hagan and met my mother, who was singing in the choir, being fed by joyful gospel hymns. And because, a double handful of generations before that, another Bradley left Ireland, feeding his dream for a new life. Had any of them—or multitudes of other relatives, teachers, or friends—fed or watered the other wolf or another patch of grass I would not be here, under this particular stretch of sky on this almost Midsummer's Night.

Across the way another streak of lightning zigzags its way toward earth. The rain is coming. The grass will grow higher.

JULY 8, 2018

"Look what I found."

The arrowhead my brother is holding between his thumb and index finger is a good two inches long and perfectly whole. It is the color of the flesh of an unripened peach. Its tip is still sharp after eons under sandy soil. Its surface is as smooth as the hundreds of strikes of stone-against-stone that created it allows it to be. It is magical.

But not so magical as to create surprise or, worse, doubt. Over the years Keith and Daddy, driving tractors that pull plows and harrows and root rakes, have unearthed hundreds of arrowheads, some smaller, a few larger, some streaked with the colors of sunset. There have been enough to prove that we are not the first people to claim this piece of dirt as our own, that its history goes far beyond the first deed I ever found in the courthouse records, that there are stories buried here that we will never know.

Arrowheads are not the only artifacts that turn up on a regular basis. There are also the iron pins used to build the stretch of Register and Glennville Railroad, begun in 1895 as a logging road, eventually becoming a common carrier before being abandoned in 1919. One of them lies on the library case by my front door. It is heavy, and flakes of rust are apt to come off in my hands if I roll it back and back as I am wont to do sometimes, just to be reminded that mine were not the first feet to travel these roads.

It, too, has a point. It, too, was created to pierce, not flesh as was the arrowhead but wood, which is, nevertheless, a kind of flesh.

There may be other artifacts hidden beneath the fields, buried in the slick mud of the ponds, lost in the impenetrable brambles of the branch that is so close to my back door I can hear rabbits rushing toward their hutches. There may be others, but these are the ones we have found—arrowheads and railroad pins.

And what occurs to me, now that I take the time—in the way of high school essay questions—to compare and contrast, is that not only do points pierce but they, well, point. They show the way.

Last Christmas some dear friends gave me the most adorable birdhouse. It has a tin roof and is painted a soft aqua color. Around the entrance hole is a tin heart with an arrow shot through à la Cupid, the courier of love. The other day, shortly after having seen Keith's new arrowhead, I was walking around the backyard and checked the birdhouse to see if I had any tenants (I don't. Not yet.), and that heart with the arrow got me thinking.

What if our long-held understanding of Cupid as an archer is all wrong? What if love isn't supposed to hurt, isn't supposed to tear muscle from bone like an arrowhead or force a hole in one thing so that it can be attached to another like a railroad pin? What if Cupid isn't aiming at someone but rather in someone's direction, showing the way for an otherwise aimless lover?

If that is true, then the lesson of the newly unearthed arrowhead is this: It is likely that the thing, the thought, the person who is going to show you the way may not be visible to the casual glance. It may be hidden somewhere in the everyday task of work. It may be turned up by the plow of an unexpected encounter. It may look, at first, like a weapon, but if you take the time to hold it, measure it, roll it between your palms, you may find that you have uncovered a set of directions to show you the way.

JULY 22, 2018

Earlier this week we got word that another member of the generation ahead of me had, in the words of Christian parlance, passed to her eternal rest. In the way of things these days, I was able to subscribe to obituary updates from the funeral home, and as I waited for the email that would tell me where and when my Aunt Jean's funeral would be held, I found myself recalling all the times that I and my friend Michael, whose office used to be next door to mine, read obituaries from the local newspaper aloud to each other.

He and I were alternately bemused and amused by the dearly departeds whose families chose to include various nicknames by which they had been known in life. John Robert "Cooter" Smith. Sally Ann "Sister" Jones. Things like that.

The relatively recent adoption of the custom of including—along with place of birth, occupation, and church membership—the activities in which the decedent took pleasure can be equally enlightening and/or thought-provoking. "Big Daddy loved quail hunting, NASCAR, and Alabama football. Roll Tide!" "Tiny enjoyed working in the yard and nothing made her happier than cooking for her family." I don't recall the obituaries of any of my grandparents including such recitations, and being a traditionalist I am glad that my grandfather's love of soap operas and the Publisher's Clearinghouse Sweepstakes is a part of his story that, at least until now, has stayed with those of us who loved him best.

And then there is the question of remembrances. It is difficult to choose, sometimes, among the multitude of suggested organizations to which contributions in memory of the deceased may be made and, having chosen, decide the appropriate amount of said contribution. You can't write the check for "an amount equal to the cost of a nice spray" and expect the people at the bank to know how much to debit your account. It was so much easier before people learned enough French to include in their family's obituaries "in lieu of flowers."

Even the standard listing of survivors—spouse, siblings, children, in-laws, grandchildren, and, depending on the view said survivors have toward paying by the word, great-grandchildren— has changed. We have moved from a simple "He is survived by…" to "Left to hold him close in warm memories are his loving wife," etc. I keep looking for one in which the enumerated survivors are "loving wife," "loving daughter," "loving sister," "loving brother," and "son." Poor son.

I am not being disrespectful, staring at my computer screen waiting for my aunt's obituary to appear and thinking such outrageous thoughts. It's called dark humor. Black humor. Gallows humor. It is the urge to make jokes about, make fun of, laugh in the face of this thing about which we know the least, this thing that frightens us most. A futile attempt to avoid the unavoidable.

The benefit of this futility is that it makes me consider the idea that none of us are survivors, but simply longer-livers. The real survivors of death are the words of kindness and the acts of mercy, the songs of joy and the peals of laughter, the moments of wonder and the expressions of love that any single human offers in any single lifetime, each of them launched like a rocket ship out into the cosmos to land someplace unknown. Each of them living forever.

AUGUST 5, 2018

It is Sunday morning. I am sitting at a restaurant table overlooking the beach at Saint Simons. The sky is the color of new chambray. The water is the color of an oft-worn, oft-washed Dickey work shirt. The entire landscape is bathed in blue.

Using the crayons provided by the kind server, I am drawing, on the back of the children's menu, a color wheel. Jackson and Chambless are watching me carefully as I demonstrate how red and blue together make purple, blue and yellow together make green, yellow and red together make orange.

They lean toward me and the color wheel as far as they can without falling out of their chairs. They stare with admiration and amazement. It is magic. "Let me try!" "I want the blue!" "Look! Look! See? It's purple!"

I have always been fascinated by color. The first tangible thing that I ever coveted was a sixty-four-pack of Crayola crayons, convinced that cornflower and salmon and goldenrod were infinitely better than plain ol' blue and red and yellow. I spent hours in my mother's sewing room arranging the endless spools of thread into sections and the sections by hue. My first term paper, written in the seventh grade for Mrs. Nell Brown, was about the use of color in interior decorating.

It was in researching that term paper, completed entirely by using the card catalog and the heavy-as-a-cinder-block *Reader's Guide to Periodical Literature*, that I first learned about the color wheel—primary and secondary colors, warm and cold colors, complementary colors. In doing so, I found explanation for the extremely strong preferences I exhibited, sometimes to my mother's chagrin, every time she and I went to the fabric store. I also armed myself to entertain my great-nephew and great-nieces in the future.

A few days later, still on the island, I am sitting high above the ground on the screened porch of the condominium where I and some co-workers are staying during a conference. It is early morning. I am surrounded by trees and shrubs and other assorted vegetation. Green. In every possible shade.

This island is one of a handful of places on the earth where I am most at home, most myself. There are moments when I long for it with an urgency that is palpable. And the image that comes to mind, that glues itself to my eyelids, is always the blue sky over the blue water. The sky and all its striations, the water in all its undulations—the blues catch my breath and hold me in their thrall.

But what I suddenly realize this morning is that here, at this place that holds so much of my heart, there are also greens. A myriad of greens. Kelly and hunter, jade and juniper, mint and avocado. There is the bright green of young pine needles and the deep, almost black green of magnolia leaves in shadow. There is the iridescent chartreuse of the marsh and the celadon of the Spanish moss. Chlorophyll, amazing in all its incarnations.

That realization morphs into the further epiphany that I probably—no, most assuredly—visualize other places, not to mention people and situations, in monochrome. I pause deliberately to allow myself to feel the disappointment, the embarrassment, the regret.

When did I become satisfied with less than the box of sixty-four? What is preventing me from reaching for aquamarine and mulberry, periwinkle and burnt sienna? And, most importantly, how quickly can I pour every single one of them out of the box and color their points down to nubs?

AUGUST 19, 2018

The way back is always longer.

The clouds are high, white as bleached sheets. Somewhere behind them is the sun, so bright that, even shielded by sunglasses, my eyes are squinting. The waves flap and overlap and tease my feet in unpredictable rhythm.

This is what I do at the beach. I walk. I play in the water, push children on boogie boards, sit in low chairs and observe the species, but mostly I walk. And this week I've done it seven times on two different islands. I've dodged jellyfish and horseshoe crabs, fishing lines and lifeguard stands, sandcastles, sand buckets, and sandwiches. I've listened to squealing toddlers and squeaking wheels and squawking seagulls. I've watched the tides move in and out, the boats move in and out, the people move in and out. All while walking. Left, right, left.

This morning I walk for the last time. The last time for this time. It is still early and the only other people on the beach are the dog-walkers, the runners, and the shell-seekers. I head north, toward the lighthouse where my friend Jason proposed to my friend Amy, toward the jetty where my friend Francie got a cut on her leg that left an inches-long scar, toward some undetermined-as-of-yet spot where I will decide to turn around and head back.

It is quiet enough, still enough that all I have to dodge is thoughts, all there is to hear is my own inner voice, all there is to watch is where I put my step. A rare moment.

I find myself considering other shorelines on which I have walked—Cape Cod in October's early morning fog, Key West in pressure cooker heat, the various islands in this chain we Georgians call ours—and I realize, just about the time I notice the sun's rapid ascent and think about turning around, that there is one thing all those walks had in common. The way back was always longer.

Not in inches or yards or miles. Not, really, even in measurable time. The way back was longer because the anticipation of what was ahead had come to an end. The way back was longer because the view was no longer novel. The way back was longer because all that walking made me tired.

My niece Kate and I were talking just the other day about reconciliation, making amends, asking forgiveness. Those are big topics these days, and there can be no argument that our tiny blue dot floating in the endless darkness of space needs a lot of all of them, but I think it's easy, when you're focusing on the big picture, to forget that the little picture is even there.

Yes, we as a nation, a state, a people have a long way to go in relating to each other, all the each others, with fairness and in love. But just as important—some might argue even more important—is how we as individuals treat the each others we know, with whom we share office space, a classroom, a history, with whom we share or used to share an address or a name. When that treatment is less than fair, less than loving, when we, literally or figuratively, walk away from our responsibilities as bearers of the divine spirit, all we do is make the way back—the only, singular, solitary way back—longer.

I've gone far past the lighthouse now, way beyond the jetty, and suddenly I know it's time to turn around and walk in the other direction. I am hot and thirsty and tired. I am not looking forward to retracing my steps. And yet I begin. One step in the opposite direction is always the beginning.

SEPTEMBER 2, 2018

Owen barks, one short squeak like a rusty screen door. As I walk through the kitchen to let him out, I notice the difference. The morning light has become, overnight, duller. Weaker. Grayer. It slants at a distinctly different angle, throwing shadows that make long stripes across the table.

Having ignored all the signs of summer moving toward an end—the change of frothy pink cotton blossoms into dense white bolls, the crunch of the first fallen sycamore leaves beneath my feet in the backyard, the burst of magenta ball bearings from the stems of the beautyberry bush—this one catches me off-guard. I sigh a petulant sigh.

It is not that I don't appreciate the ability to walk outside without my sunglasses fogging up. It is not that I don't like boots and blue jeans. It is not that I can't get excited about football. I do and I can. But for a long time, the end of summer has been for me, more than anything else, the harbinger of winter. I start feeling the cold long before it gets here, drawing my shoulders up to my ears the minute the wind picks up, shivering involuntarily at the first long-range forecast.

I am not proud.

Normally I am the one admonishing others to pay attention, to be alert, to notice the moment. And here I am, once a year, losing sight of what is in dread of what is to come.

I am, as I said, not proud.

There are, according to the best statistics, over a quarter million people in Georgia alone who are visually impaired. For at least some of them, glasses or contact lenses or the best Lasik surgeon in the world wouldn't do any good. They are completely, irreversibly blind.

That statistic frightens me. And not just because my near-sightedness can sometimes make it difficult to read road signs or the credits on a movie screen. It frightens me because I know without the help of any statistician that there are a great many more people who are equally, if differently, blind. People who can't see the wealth in which they stand, the beauty in which they walk, the incredible grace in which they live and move and have their being. People who are so madly working for an indeterminate future that they are immune to the poignancy of today.

I don't want to be a part of that statistic, not even in the single instance of the apprehension of winter. I want to be the statistic that has 20/20 vision, that sees every leaf, every smile, every shade of every color right now exactly as it is and, in seeing it, gasps at the wonder, marvels at the magic, weeps at the preciousness of the singularity.

Toward that end, I am not unaware that, like Dorothy with her ruby slippers, I have within myself the power to make that happen. Maybe not by clicking my heels together, but by being very still and repeating over and over again to myself what I know to be true.

I pause. Briefly. Look again at the light thrown onto the table through the window blinds. It isn't dull; it is soft. It isn't weak; it is soothing. It isn't gray; it is silver—rippling and shimmering like the surface of a lake in autumn.

Winter will come. It will be cold. I will shiver and watch my breath form miniature clouds. I will stare at the ice lace on the windows and make up a name for the pattern. I will look at all the empty branches and imagine them as letters in another language. I will make a sincere effort not to complain.

For now, for today, I will watch the last summer light and see with clear vision only what is, not what will be. Boiled peanuts, goldenrod, and combines rolling over fields with the precision of a marching band. Late tomatoes, early asters, and battalions of school buses filled with children smelling of sweat and ketchup and glue. Hot pink sunsets, bruise-colored muscadines, and the horizon-wide view of summer turning to fall.

SEPTEMBER 16, 2018

The clouds are thick and dark and close enough to the ground that a crane, I think, could reach the plug that holds all the water inside. I am hoping that the center holds until I get home, but I have driven this stretch of Highway 301 enough times—thousands of times—to know that somewhere between Jimps and the intersection with Highway 46 that plug will pop.

I am paying more attention than I might ordinarily because, of course, Hurricane Florence is bearing down on the east coast and because, of course, today—Tuesday—is the first anniversary of the arrival of Hurricane Irma in southeast Georgia. In just a couple of weeks, the second anniversary of Hurricane Matthew will be upon us. Who wouldn't be watching the sky?

In the distance there is a rumbling that could be thunder or could be the massive trucks that are my multiple and constant companions on this highway that I remember as a two-lane black-top and that Daddy is quick to remind me he remembers as a dirt road. Keeping my eyes on my lane, I try to sneak a look at the dashboard to see if the headlights have come on.

Suddenly, just to the right, behind a convenience store that looks as though it may have already lost power, a bolt of lightning throws itself toward the ground like the spear of the gods the Greeks thought it was. Before I can start counting the lapse of time between lightning and thunder, the thunder itself fills the car. Like the radio bass turned up too loud.

"Wow!" The exclamation is involuntary. "That was close."

And then, before I can release my caught breath, I smell it.

The lightning. Like electrical sparks.

I have never smelled lightning before. Never—I guess—been quite this close, but somehow I know exactly what it is. I will look it up later, just to be sure, but I don't need to. I know.

The rain starts. I drive through it. By the time I get home it has stopped, but the clouds are still hovering, still pendulous. Still humming with the threat of bad weather. And I can't resist going outside to walk around in it. Owen and I circle the yard over and over, brave enough to taunt the clouds but not so imprudent as to get too far from cover.

If there is any punctuation mark to my days it is this—walking the perimeter of Sandhill and watching the sky change from day to night. There isn't another human being for at least half a mile. My view of the sunset is impeded only by treetops, and I keep track of the movement of the earth through the seasons by finding which tree is the last one to hold a glimmer of light before the sun is completely gone.

Tonight, the smell of lightning still in my head, I can see only a thin strip of bright burgundy. The clouds are blocking the rest of the light show—bright pink, glowing peach, gleaming orange. I can't see them, but they are there. I know.

I am struck at that moment by two things. The first is that there is great value in knowing. The colors of the sunset, through every season, in every shade of the spectrum, I know from careful, attentive, consistent observation. That observation creates recognition and recognition creates appreciation and appreciation creates love.

The second thing is that there is also great value in the discovery of something new to know. The smell of lightning is now a part of my experience, my history, my story because of presence.

Presence leads to awareness and awareness leads to appreciation and appreciation, as I said, leads to love.

If, then, what the world needs now is more love, I think we

could start with more knowing. The kind that comes from observation and presence, the kind that comes from deep breaths and stillness, the kind that comes from smelling lightning.

SEPTEMBER 30, 2018

On February 7, 2018, *USA Today* predicted that the Atlanta Braves would finish in third place in the National League East. Even the hometown *Journal-Constitution* predicted no better than a tie for third place, forecasting a 76–86 record. There were a lot of people who didn't have much hope.

A few months ago at the quarterly meeting of the Georgia Humanities Council, I heard about the recent completion of Georgia's Footsteps of Dr. Martin Luther King, Jr. Trail. One of the stops on the trail is the bronze statue of Dr. King unveiled on the grounds of the State Capitol in August 2017. Also on the trail is the First African Baptist Church in Dublin. It was there that a fifteen-year-old Martin King gave his first public speech as the winner of the Colored Elks Club of Georgia oratory contest. The speech was titled "The Negro and the Constitution." After delivering that speech, on the trip back to Atlanta, he was—for the first time—asked to relinquish his seat to a white passenger and step to the back of the bus.

I was sitting at the council meeting next to Ira Jackson. He is tall and lean and could be mistaken for a baseball player. He has a James Earl Jones-type voice. At the end of the report on the trail, Ira sat back in his chair, stretched out his long legs, and began to speak.

"When I was growing up in Atlanta," he said, "and I walked downtown, across the square of the State Capitol, I walked under the shadow of the statues of those other men." He paused. "I could not imagine that the day would come when Dr. King would be among them. Hope," he said in his soft, deep voice, "is hard."

I felt my breath catch in my throat and I knew he was right. But I wasn't sure why. Over the following weeks the phrase kept rolling over and over in my mind as I tried to figure out what it meant. I thought about it every time I heard someone say, "I hope this meeting doesn't last long" or "I hope it doesn't rain for the party," and decided that that kind of hope, the kind relegated to wishing and longing, is no more useful than letters to Santa Claus.

Hope is supposed to be more than that. It is, in New Testament terms, an anchor for the soul, the tangible thing that holds the vessel steady in the calm and propels it through the storm. Hope isn't bound by the past or by predictions.

On March 29, 2018, opening day, the Atlanta Braves began the season with a twenty-five-man roster and hope. And a lot of unexpected things happened over the next six months. Like a twenty-year-old rookie hitting lead-off homers in five straight games. Like a veteran player in his thirteenth season making his first All-Star team. Like a pitcher coming back after three Tommy John surgeries.

And on September 22, 2018, with eight games still to play, the Atlanta Braves clinched the pennant.

I don't know if Ira Jackson was watching that game. I was. And I couldn't help thinking that the 2018 Braves and the fight for racial equality have something in common, as do every other thought, activity, and endeavor of the human experience. They have in common the undeniable truth that hope is hard, but it is equally hard to resist.

OCTOBER 14, 2018

It is Friday afternoon. It has been a long week. What am I doing at Walmart?

I push the buggy purposefully. The object of my quest is a car phone charger. I stop in front of a section marked "Android phone accessories" where all of the displayed items appear to be for iPhones. Utilizing my superior deductive capabilities, I move to the section marked "iPhone accessories" to find that, as I suspected, all of these items are for Androids. There are, however, no chargers.

I circle back to the electronics department checkout, where one Walmart employee is engaged in making a laborious return of some kind and a second is held captive by the flirtatious conversation of a middle-aged customer in cut-off jeans. I wait.

A third employee materializes and walks right past me toward a couple browsing the no-contract cell phone display. "Can I help you?" she asks them. "Yeh," the female customer laughs, "if you can show us a cheap one!" This could, it is clear, take a while.

I take a couple of steps toward them. "Excuse me." I lean into the huddle the three of them have made. "I hate to interrupt, but could you just tell me where car chargers are?" With a finger-point from the employee and an assurance that "That's all right, honey; we ain't in no hurry" from the customer, I resume my single-minded pursuit.

About halfway to the rack to which I've been directed, two young women step out in front of me, not quite blocking my path but making it clear that they want me to stop. "Are you a teacher?" the blonde one asks. "A principal?"

I see where this is going. They think they recognize me. They have seen my photo in the newspaper, or maybe they've seen me in court and just can't place me. "I'm a prosecuting attorney," I offer.

They look at each other, smile broadly, and nod, confirming something, but I'm not sure what. "We were watching you and you're so"—she pauses to find a word—"powerful."

I nearly burst out laughing. "We could tell that you're somebody who is…" She stops. She is suddenly embarrassed. So am I. None of us knows what to do next.

"Can I ask you something?" The other one, petite and with the intense gaze of the dangerously naive, steps closer and begins to tell me, in words falling over each other like puppies in a kennel, of her current legal troubles. Nothing awful. What my colleagues and I call misdemeanor stupidity.

With the last embarrassing detail shared, she gazes up at me hopefully. I am, I suddenly realize, so much taller than she. "I'm really sorry," I tell her, "but I can't give you legal advice." I explain that my job as a sworn officer of the state prohibits me from giving legal advice to individual citizens.

She looks confused. She thought I was powerful. She thought I could fix her problem or at least make it less of one.

Unfortunately, the illusion of power is just that. An illusion. Regardless of what they saw when they looked at me, I can't fix things, I can't change what happened, I can't save people. It is not a matter of effort or expertise, knowledge or skill set, tools or timing. It is a matter of identity. And I am not a savior.

The blonde reaches out to pull her friend gently away and says to me, "It's okay. Really." Then, to her friend, "I didn't think she could help, but she listened. She listened all the way through."

They back away, smiling and waving in the disarming way of people who don't know they have created an awkward situation, smiling and waving like grade-schoolers off on a great adventure, smiling and waving as though this was just an ordinary Walmart encounter between neighbors or school chums, as though it was not a hinge in the cosmos, a point on which something important bent at a new angle.

I am still for what feels like a long time. I wonder if maybe it's not that power is an illusion but that it is just far subtler in its manifestation than we realize. I wonder if maybe we are all far more powerful than we've ever imagined. I wonder if maybe taking time, paying attention, listening might be what fixes things, what changes things, what saves people.

It is Friday afternoon. I am at Walmart listening all the way through.

OCTOBER 28, 2018

Ossabaw. Say it out loud. It will start with a rumble at the back of your throat, a rumble that reminds you of when you sat in front of your grandmother's oscillating fan and aahed into its blades for as long as your breath would allow. It will slip into the cave of your mouth where the air slides through your teeth with a hiss like a tire going flat. It will end with a burst, your lips separating abruptly as the whole word escapes into the universe, lifting and floating, dipping and diving like an osprey over the waves.

Ossabaw. Live oaks dripping Spanish moss, vines as thick as a man's arms winding like cobras up the trunks of loblolly pines, garden statuary hidden under green grown thick and high. The mansion, majestic even in its decay, doors thrown open to catch the breeze off the marsh and to welcome the guests who move slowly, reverently through its rooms. In its quiet and somberness it exudes a different kind of magic.

I am here, in this place cordoned off from the rest of the world, through the generosity of a friend. I want to sit silently on the trunk of one of the fallen trees and stare out at the marsh, flashing gold in the autumn sun, and simultaneously to walk as fast as I can down every dirt road and trail and hallway I can find, breathing in the stories that I am sure are lingering in every crevice.

When it is time to eat, time for roast pig and cheese grits and sweet tea, we sit at big round tables scattered across the front yard. I pull a journal out of my backpack to take notes, to scribble down the things I do not want to forget.

We, all and each of us guests, came over by boat, the only way to get to Ossabaw. There is no bridge, no airfield, no helipad. I stood at the bow of the powerboat, beside Captain Joe, and watched the water split in front of us, rolling back like a liquid zipper. Three or four times we passed other boats going in the opposite direction, and each time Joe pulled back on the throttle and turned the boat just slightly to meet the other boat's wake at an angle.

I write that down and stop mid-sentence. It is a metaphor for something. I don't know what yet.

Hours later, sated with roast pig and cheese grits and sweet tea, I am back on that same boat, leaving in my own wake the Sicilian donkeys, the Peter Pan Garden, the tabby houses, the catalysts for what I can tell already is a difference I will feel for a long time before I name it. Dark clouds are advancing quickly; Captain Joe makes a quick announcement: "Hold on. It's going to be choppy."

And it is. Standing at the bow again, I can see that he never pulls back on the throttle. He never turns into any of the choppy waves that keep us company all the way back to the marina on the mainland. He drives us straight ahead and into the waves. We beat the rain by about five minutes.

It is days later that I figure it out. The metaphor. It is not nature of which we must be afraid. Not dark clouds or rain or waves created by either. It is people and their machines and the wake they leave behind.

Whether it is magical Ossabaw or the hurricane-ravaged panhandle of Florida or my own heart, it can withstand the seasons, the tides, the storms. But none of them is immune to the malicious act, the intentional injury, the conscious neglect of human beings. If we are to be stewards, then, whether on behalf of ourselves or the people and places we treasure, we must learn when to pull back on the throttle, when to turn into the wave.

NOVEMBER 11, 2018

I have often proclaimed, with only a bit of irony, that I can drive to Macon in my sleep or, in the alternative, that my car can get there without any assistance on my part. I've been driving that westward trek on a regular basis since I was seventeen years old, since before I-16 was completed, since the route included downtown Soperton.

I, like anyone who has ever driven it more than once, have complained about the boredom, the soporific monotony of one hundred miles of straight flatness, made worse by the recent barbarous removal of pine trees from the median. However, that sameness has often been a blessing on days when my overloaded brain, my exhausted heart were incapable of the advanced thinking required by curves and turns, crests and hills.

On those days, the rhythmic thumping of tires on concrete, the motionlessness of my wrist dangling over the top of the steering wheel, the stillness inside the steel cage into which I have buckled myself have been not an irritant but a balm.

Over the last few months a monumental construction project at the confluence of I-16 and I-75 has demanded a great deal more attention than that intersection has required in the previous forty-four years in which I have navigated its knot. I can no longer simply veer left or right. The DOT has inserted a detour, unavoidable changes in direction, signs and flashing lights and orange and white barrels clustered together into a rat's nest of caution and warning.

As a result, when I drove to Macon last week for a meeting, I made my way over the Ocmulgee River not with one hand dangling like a duchess awaiting a courtier's kiss but with both fists gripping the steering wheel like an action hero holding on to the ledge of a skyscraper with nothing but twenty stories of air between her and the pavement.

That night, after the meeting, I had dinner with a friend in a quiet restaurant with small tables, dim lights, and servers who moved with admirable stealth to remove and replace china and silverware. It is easy to talk in such a place. The words flow, the topics slide into and out of each other. There is nothing linear about the stories and yet they all make sense.

At some point, one of us must have brought up the drive each had made to get there and the drive each would have to make to get back home. Mention was made of the hazards of night driving—detours, car trouble, and kamikaze deer—and my friend's dislike of driving after dark. She would, she told me, stay the night in Macon. I would, I told her, go on home.

We talked about a lot of things at that table in that restaurant. Big things. Important things. But in the days that followed the one thing that kept coming back to me was the idea of detours.

It's bad enough, I thought, when the detour is a literal one—a blockade across the road with a big red arrow pointing in a direction you had no intention of going—but it is far worse when it is the other kind. The loss of a job, a relationship, or a purpose. In those cases there is no GPS or Waze to quell the disorientation or offer the security of someone else's prior experience. When that which gives you your sense of identity walks out the door or sends you walking, there is nothing that will make you feel anything other than lost.

I've been lost. More than once. I have come up on detours so suddenly that I had no time to hit the brakes but, instead, crashed head-on into the barrier where I had to sit, alone and scared, until my wits returned and I remembered that there is a gear called reverse.

From those experiences and the nagging replay of that restaurant conversation, this is what I've figured out: The purpose of the detour is to protect you from something you can't see, from the danger from which you would not have been able to protect yourself. And, though it may delay the journey, if you follow the signs, you will always make it to your original destination. With unclenched fists.

NOVEMBER 25, 2018

There are no easy harvests.

There are good harvests, occasionally even bountiful harvests, and disappointing harvests. There are harvests that translate into profit and those that evaporate into losses so large that only a fool would ever harrow another field, plant another seed. There are long harvests, short harvests, early harvests, and late harvests, but there are no easy harvests.

I am reminded of this truth as the rain beats the roof and the windows of my house like artillery shells. On three sides I am neighbored by picked-over cotton fields, the skinny stalks naked but for the occasional misshapen boll that somehow avoided the maul of the cotton picker rumbling over it weeks before. If these fields were all there were, their emptiness would be comforting, a soothing reminder of the cycle of the seasons, but a few miles away there are other fields, still full, still waiting. And it just keeps raining.

The rain, though, it must be said, hasn't been the only thing delaying the gathering of a crop that, at its peak, brought out the hopefulness in my family's farmers. First, it was the hurricane that blustered its way across Georgia, arriving at these fields with enough residual wind to rip the bolls from the grip of the stiff brown calyxes that held them like cupped palms.

Then it was equipment problems: bad bearings, worn spindle bushings. And now it is the rain. Once it stops—whenever that is—it may take a week or more for the land to dry out enough to hold up the 70,000-pound cotton picker.

There are no easy harvests.

In 1979 Hurricane David arrived precisely at the moment the corn was ready to be picked. Acres of tall earth-colored shocks were flattened. We, all of us, spent days walking down each row, lifting each stalk, breaking off each fully matured ear of corn that would have been wasted had we not, and tossing all of them into piles that we would later transfer to the bed of the worn-out pickup truck I had driven as a senior in high school.

When all the stalks had been picked clean like roadkill, we stood in front of the combine, its header raised like big yellow teeth opened around a gaping mouth where gears ground so loudly that the diesel motor, usually deafening, was little more than a hum. One by one we tossed the ears into the darkness, underhand like pitching a softball. One by one the ears disappeared and then reappeared, stripped of the hard gold kernels, out the other end as though the combine was defecating.

High above us, the kernels poured into the hopper and slowly, slowly, slowly the piles that we had made, the fruits of the labors not just of our post-hurricane days but of all the days since the first bright green sprouts had split the crusty earth, grew smaller and smaller until there was nothing left to throw.

There are no easy harvests.

Somewhere along the way we got the idea that reaping was

easier than sowing. That once the seed was planted, the idea expressed, the introductions made, all the hard work was over. We forgot or simply dismissed the idea that in every attempt to build, to create, to discover there must be toil. In every effort toward growth there will be opposition.

We denigrate ourselves and all who have come before us when we focus our attention on eliminating the struggle.

There are no easy harvests.

DECEMBER 9, 2018

And, suddenly, the sawtooth oak is gold, dripping with leaves heavy with three days' rain. Leaves that somehow manage to shimmer in the infinitesimal amount of light coming through the clouds. Leaves that point like fingers toward the ground to which they are falling even before they let go.

But, of course, there is nothing sudden about it. For weeks the chlorophyll has been dying, Camille-like—fading slowly, sighing imperceptibly. Way before Thanksgiving the annual carpeting of the backyard with leaves I have no intention of raking began, the soft crinkle under the sound of the car's tires reminding me of the cellophane twisted around peppermint. Way before the time change and the nightly deer rodeo in the driveway and the irritation with which I took off the dry cleaner's plastic from my winter coat, the leaves were changing.

There was a time when I would have attributed the sensation of suddenness—Suddenly the tree is gold!—with my failure to notice, to observe, to pay attention. I would have chided, scolded, berated myself—out loud and in the presence of the tree—for all manner of human shortcoming. By the time I was done I'd have made a good case that I was responsible for everything from the egg that rolled out of the nest in the mailbox to the Braves' ouster from the playoffs to climate change.

There was that time, but it is not now. Because now, after living enough years and experiencing enough suddenlys, I understand that the sensation of suddenness has less to do with the event itself and more to do with the emotion felt in response to it.

Every mother knows that her infant son will eventually be sixteen and driving trucks and going on dates, and every mother, despite her promises to herself and her equally evolved friends, eventually posts on Facebook: "Cherish every moment. In the blink of an eye, they'll be gone." Suddenly.

Every single Bulldawg fan who entered Mercedes-Benz stadium last Saturday afternoon knew that college football games last about three hours, give or take an injury time-out or two. And every single Bulldawg fan, as the clock ran down, gasped in disappointment that the magical season was over. Suddenly.

Somewhere around ten o'clock the morning after I notice the tree, I stumble into the kitchen, my bare feet feeling both the smoothness and the coldness of the wood floor. I have been sick all week, knew last night that I'd not make it to church, had set no alarm in the hope that extra sleep might make me well. It didn't. It still feels as though someone has stuffed an Army blanket inside my head.

I squint my eyes against the light that comes through the big bay window and—suddenly—realize what day it is. The first Sunday of Advent.

Like the leaves, there is nothing sudden about its arrival. For months we have moved through the church calendar—Lent then Easter then Pentecost then Ordinary Time—on the way to these four quick weeks before Christmas. It is suddenly the first Sunday in Advent only because of the feelings it elicits: Frustration at the absence of a tree and no idea when or if one will get put up. Wistfulness over the passage of another year in which things done and undone did not match up to my to-do list. Fatigue from the illness that simply will not go away.

I will at least, I decide, get out the Advent wreath. It takes a while to find the candles where I put them last year. They slide out of the box, little spears of wax breaking off the sides, onto the table where the wreath with its four perfect holes awaits. One by one I set them in, straight and tall and fragile, and it is only as the last one takes its place that I remember.

The first candle, the one we light today, is the candle of hope. Hope that kept a people alive for thousands of years of enslavement. Hope that changed the world forever from a barn in Bethlehem. Hope that exists today even in frustration and wistfulness and fatigue.

I stare at the unlit candle, its wick dark and curved, and—suddenly—it is Christmas.

DECEMBER 23, 2018

This town. Every morning I drive toward it and watch it appear in the fold of the sky, at the edge of the horizon. Spread from the center like spilled milk, it reaches out to greet me, its permeable edge drawing me in.

This town is my town. I was born, taught, and preached to in one after another of its red brick buildings. Under its pines and magnolias, its humid skies, its drawling voices I learned to breathe, to read, to believe.

This town is the answer to the question I've been asked a thousand times. Where are you from? A simple inquiry made heavy by the weight of a stranded preposition. On this morning, a few days before Christmas, I am asking myself that question. Where am I from? Not what point of geography do I call my provenance, but what is my source.

While I read the newspaper, check phone messages, review

my calendar, my mind wanders. I remember, with the perspective of an adult, what it was like to grow up here. This was the town where strangers called tourists were always allowed to merge into traffic and given a smile and a wave. This was the town where families named Minkovitz and Seligman and Rudderman operated stores where my family and I happily shopped for Buster Brown shoes and Villager skirts. This was the town that desegregated its public schools without any of the violence that was broadcast into our homes from other towns on the evening news, even as its Confederate monument stood silently on the courthouse square.

The last memory comes into sharper focus. It is the first day of desegregation. I am in fifth grade at Mattie Lively. Neither I nor any of my classmates know what to expect. Our teacher, Julia Trapnell, her shirtwaist dress starch-pressed and trim, opens the classroom door and a girl, a black girl, walks in. "Children," Mrs. Trapnell says, "this is Kathy Love. She is going to be in our class."

No one says anything. "Kathy." It is clear Mrs. Trapnell is speaking to me, not the new girl. "I'd like for you to sit at the table in the back with the new Kathy while she gets adjusted." I pick up my books and silently move to the rear of the room, waiting for Kathy Love to join me.

I look out the window, the window of my office that, when I was in fifth grade, would have been the storeroom of the Buggy and Wagon building, and I try to remember more about that day, the day ten-year-old Kathy Love, all on her own, changed this town. But I can't.

What I can remember, though, is a day about a year ago. I'd been invited to speak to the local Board of Realtors. We ate civic club lunch food and then I was introduced by my friend the program chairman and then I spoke for the allotted fifteen to twenty minutes about writing and words and power. When I was done, lots of kind people—some of whom I knew, some of whom I didn't—came up to shake my hand and tell me thank you.

One of those people was a young black man—tall and lean, with an easy smile. He offered his hand with an enthusiasm that made me know he had found the right profession. "I am Reginald Love," he offered.

"Are you from here?" I asked. "I went to school with some Loves."

And, upon hearing that he was, in fact, a Bulloch County Love, I proceeded for some inexplicable reason to tell him the story, the story of the day I met Kathy Love. By the time I finished his smile had transformed to a grin.

"I've heard that story," he said. "My family tells it, the story that Kathy was given a helper, a friend."

I gasped, gripped his hand in both my own while tears welled in my eyes. "Thank you," I offered. They were the only words worth saying.

Every town has its stories, stories that rise from its people and then fall back down like rain upon their shoulders to bring forth more. It is important to tell them.

Where am I from? I am from this town. This town is my town. This town is me.

Thoughts in Benediction

Summer 2019: In just over two months I have spent nine days on four islands in three states. It is the most concentrated time I have ever spent in sight of the ocean. I have drawn from the sand, brushed clean, and brought home as souvenirs two pure white seagull feathers, one pink roseate spoonbill feather, one sliver of moon shell, two fragments of sand dollar, and a shard of what must have been a scallop shell, half an inch thick and the size of a computer mouse. Artifacts.

With the shell fragment in my hand I am remembering Saturday morning on Tybee.

It is long past sunrise when I start my walk. The sky is bright and clear, with just enough haze to blur the horizon. The shell-seekers and dog-walkers are gone; the young parents struggling with plastic toys and sunscreen and the teenagers struggling with nothing save their Frisbee game are just beginning to seep their way from the hotels, the condos, the public parking lots. I am not alone, but neither am I crowded.

There are lots of seagulls this morning. Their voices, unlike that of the birds that accompany me on my walks at Sandhill, produce no songs, only incessant chatter. They talk over each other like my friends and me when we gather for our annual beach visit. There is so much to share and so little time in which to share it.

Because the tide is going out, I walk farther than usual, past the lighthouse, past the rows of rocks that run from dunes to ocean and always remind me of the plates along a dragon's back. When I turn around I realize the tide has ebbed to low, very low.

I also realize that it is a lot hotter than when I started. If I am going to benefit from the breeze coming from the slapping waves, I will have to move farther out, farther from the sea oats and rows of resort chairs and matching umbrellas, farther from the landmarks that show me the way back.

It is probably twenty minutes later when I stop to take my bearings. There is a swath of beach the length of a football field between me and the houses and condominiums that mark the invisible but obvious line beyond which the ocean will not allow humans to lay claim. And, though the oyster shells and dead jellyfish and abandoned sand toys at my feet are perfectly clear, the buildings are a blur. I can say with a fair amount of certainty, however, that I've never seen them before, that I've never been this far down the beach, and that I'm not going to find my way back unless I move away from the companionship of the water and the comfort of the breeze.

Walking becomes more difficult as I leave the hard, water-packed selvage of earth and move toward the dunes. My feet sink and rise, sink and rise, sink and—with increasing effort—rise. The sand slips and slides beneath my shoes. According to the step counter on my phone I've walked about three miles, not a lot under normal circumstances, but these are not normal circumstances. It is hot. Very hot. And I am very thirsty. I lick my lips and taste salt.

I can feel the muscles in my calves, my thighs, my back as they contract, a rhythmic stinging with each step. My breath, though, is deep and steady. My heart is doing its job of pumping blood and oxygen. With every pulse it adds to its record of uninterrupted service. Over three *billion* beats.

In the sweltering heat, I am remembering now the coolness of the dark room where I held my arms over my head for twenty minutes while a machine that looked like a giant book splayed open whirred around me in a wide circle. I am remembering the sticky white electrodes on my exposed chest and the octopus tentacle cords. I am remembering the machines, the needles, the syringes. The sound of the doctor's voice. "There is one thing, though."

What has it been? Two years?

Over the sound of the surf and the birds I hear my own voice. I realize that I am speaking. Out loud. To the doctor. To myself. To the ocean and the sky. "No, nice young doctor," I am saying as I plod through the sand. "Not one thing. Many things. There are thousands of artifacts hidden within this heart, beneath the surface, behind the mask. I have not found them all, but I am still digging."

Just ahead I see the distinctive roof line of my temporary dwelling. "Thank you," I whisper to my heart and press on.

Artifacts. People, places, moments that begin in momentary consciousness, burrow into memory. Disturbing earth, leaving scars. Eventually buried by wind and rain, pushed deeper and deeper beneath the surface. By time. All but forgotten.

Then, one day, something prompts you to dig.

So you do. And you uncover something. You don't know, at first, what it is. You can't tell at first look, at first touch. You must be gentle. With the object and with yourself.

Hold it tenderly. Blow away the dirt with a whisper. Notice the sharp edges, the smooth curves, the colors that change in the light. This is how to handle a treasure. How to discover that the sharp ends of arrowheads and railroad spikes were made to pierce *and* point, how to learn that grace is made tangible in a grapefruit, how to unravel the mystery that a penny can, if only for a moment, vanquish death.

It is not simply what you find. It is what you find out.

Finding the words is not always easy. Giving language to what I have seen or heard, thought or felt, remembered or forgotten takes time. And effort. It is, I have learned, the task of a life-

time, this searching for quarter-inch truth, this sifting for artifacts.

Acknowledgments

Not everyone takes the time to read an author's acknowledgments. This fact is difficult for me to fathom. It appears, though, that some readers do not understand the essential nature of the brief moment in which the author takes a deep breath, blinks back a tear, and expresses gratitude to the people and places that made it possible for her to produce, without losing her mind, the words that now appear in print. Some few, however, do read acknowledgments, and so, the first thank-you is to them. Thank you for noticing the names of these people I love, for giving them just a tiny bit of attention, which is not anywhere near enough for what they have given me.

And thank you, too, for reading this book. All of it, part of it, any of it. That you have spent even one moment of what Mary Oliver called "your one wild and precious life" reading my words makes me want to fall at your feet and weep. Writing is hard, but it is the only vocation I have found worthy of my one wild and precious life.

As always, I offer deepest inexplicable gratitude to my beloved families. I'm considering writing something one day in which a character is named K.R. Bradley, thereby giving each and every one of you a literary namesake. Until then, know this: Whether what binds us together is DNA or memories or both, you well know that without you I am a lot like sounding brass and tinkling cymbals.

A special thank-you to my niece Kate Bradley Viana, who carries the word gene and never lets me get by with less than the truth. Without her late-night Skype call from Ukraine, there would not have been a first book and then, of course, no second or third.

Speaking of Kate, she tells me all the time that I have a million friends. She exaggerates. But I do have a lot. There are the Buckeyes, the Prosecuties, the Board of Directors, and a whole crowd of people who are content to be known simply by their given names. You are, each and all, cherished, and the fact that you believe in me is the greatest gift a girl could ever receive.

Sarah Domet, your encouragement and friendship are among the biggest reasons this book exists. I will be ever grateful.

And finally, not because it's the traditional thing to do but because it is necessary, thank you to Marc Jolley and the sweethearts at Mercer University Press. The first time Marc and I met, I knew that he was a man serious about words and that he could be trusted with mine. As for the little staff that could—Marsha and Mary Beth and Jenny and Heather—you are, quite simply, amazing.

—Kathy A. Bradley
Sandhill
March 2022